getting Waisted

A Survival Guide to **BEING FAT** in a Society That LOVES THIN

MONICA PARKER

Health Communications, Inc.
Deerfield Beach, Florida

www.hcibooks.com

For Gilles and Remy— TMD always and forever.

Contents: Nibbles, Morsels & Big Bites

Acknowledgments

I have only endless gratitude to my truly beautiful husband, Gilles, and my remarkable son and daughter-in-law, Remy and Lise. Deep thanks to my indefatigable sister, Gerda Sless, for giving me permission to paint her from my twelve-year-old-self's brush. Dear, generous, Deborah Burgess for so much; the equally spectacular Noreen Halpern and Kevin Murphy; and Karen and Stewart Tanz for their belief in me. To Denise Deutsch for slogging through snowstorm after snowstorm to help with whatever computer disaster was at hand. To the best friends and family I could ever dream of. I hope you all know how much you mean to me. For continuously offering the help I didn't always know I needed: Michael Elliot, Perry Zimel, Linda Chester, Nancey Silvers, Betty Gaertner, Ellen Bergeron, Gary Ottoson, Wendy Crewson, Allan Royal, Suzanne McKenney, Kerrie Keane, Arlene Sarner, Shelby and Lee Chaden. For being there to offer direction and assistance: Michelle Shepherd, Sascha Alper, Aviva Leighton, Catherine McCartney, Heather Summerhayes, Jillian Medoff, Shannon Final, Darlene Chan, MJ Rose, Joanna DeGeneres,

Margot Allin, Veronique Vial, Jason Jones, Martyn Burke, and so many more. Special acknowledgement to everyone at HCI Books, and heartfelt thanks to my editor, Christine Belleris, and to the PR wonder Kim Weiss.

Introduction

Normally when I introduce myself, I like to be well-dressed. When I am writing, however, I usually look like a Chechen peasant woman on her journey to the local dump in the dead of winter: I sport an oversized T-shirt that is nearly sheer from too many washings (but is at the peak of softness), accented with a faded sarong tied over a pair of tattered sweatpants, tucked into floppy-eared house slippers. This glorious outfit is accompanied by a pill-y wool shawl that, if recollection serves right, was once deep blue, but after so much wear and tear is no longer any known color. This is what I wear, so that I can't bolt. There is a frayed "leave all deliveries" sign on my door because this outfit is not even fit for rejecting Jehovah's Witnesses. Therefore, I'd like to apologize for meeting you like this because I am as far from "runway ready" as I could possibly be. I can't even offer you cake to make up for the image I have surely branded on your ocular nerve. It's apparently frowned upon in this gluten-free hemisphere. Aw hell, if I could magically share the gooiest, yummiest triple-tiered chocolate cake with all of you who have come here to

1

get to know me and my thoughts on why dieting doesn't work, it would be my pleasure to dish it up. But seeing as cake teleportation is still nothing but cheap talk, you'll have to read along as I dish it up in a whole other way.

This book is all about my desperate attempt to get thin, aided and abetted by a whole whack of diet hucksters and hustlers, all promising the fastest fix to a better new me. I could hardly wait to throw my hard-earned money at their feet. And, like Alice, I drank their elixirs and became tiny. What they didn't tell me was—it wouldn't last.

The need to alter my body started from the moment my little yellow head, followed by my chubby, jaundiced body, appeared on the planet. This is the tale of that fat baby growing into a fat adolescent and continuing to grow and grow, until I became me: a fat woman. Along the way, I disappointed almost everyone on my path as I gained and lost and gained, over and over, fueled by my need to be liked, loved, and wooed. Unconsciously, I developed a personality resistant to failure; like a child's Bop Bag, I stood up each time I was knocked down, and each time I grew stronger, funnier, and more powerful in my conviction that I was going to dazzle the world on my own terms. But this didn't happen without a few scratches, dents, and dings along the way.

This is also about an unexpected and unimaginable love story that should give pause to every man and woman, of all shapes and sizes, who don't think this could happen for them. It can. It happened for me.

As a way of thanking you for coming along on my journey, it's my pleasure to offer you a cup of politically incorrect deliciousness, the most dangerous recipe in the world:

Five-Minute **CHOCOLATE** Mug Cake

4 T flour

4 T sugar

2 T cocoa

1 egg

3 T milk

3 T oil

3 T chocolate chips (optional)

A small smash of vanilla extract

1 large microwave-safe coffee mug

(This yummy dessert can serve two if you need to feel virtuous.)

Add dry ingredients to mug and mix well. Add the egg and mix thoroughly.

Pour in the milk and oil and mix well.

Add the chocolate chips (if using), and vanilla extract, and mix again.

Put mug in microwave and cook for three minutes at 1000 watts.

The cake will rise over the top of the mug but don't be alarmed!

Allow to cool a little, then tip out onto plate, if desired. EAT!

And why is this *the* most dangerous cake recipe in the world? Because now you are all only five minutes away from chocolate cake at any time of the day or night! Life is tough. It's either tranquilizers or cake.

1

My Parents Did It Once

The first diet ✦ **Mother's milk**

Cost ✦ **A lifelong carb-loving appetite**

Weight lost ✦ **None**

Weight gained ✦ **Zygote to zaftig at warp speed**

was born in Glasgow, Scotland. I weighed six and a half pounds. One hour later I weighed sixty-two pounds. Alright, maybe this is a slight exaggeration, but only about the time. My fat cells did start expanding at warp speed from the minute I exited the womb, and latched on to my mother's breast. I've been on a slippery slope ever since. There were no twisted demons on the inside eating away at me; it was just me, on the outside, eating. I have no idea what was in that breast milk. I am pretty sure it was loaded with wiener schnitzel, potato dumplings, and heavy cream. My addiction was born on the same day I was, and it didn't take long for my family to begin grabbing my thighs, pinching my cheeks, and exclaiming what an adorable little porker I was.

My mother missed her much older children; they had become separated during the war in their escape from Hitler and his merry marauding men. My mother, Queen Elizabeth (that's what I called her because her name was Elizabeth and she really believed she was royalty), had been married before but he wasn't worthy, so she was a single, bridge-playing, mother of two teenagers when the Nazis demanded she leave Austria. "It's not personal, you are Jewish. If you stay, we will find you, then we'll torture you and kill you or you could try to leave when we're not looking and take your chances."

She took her chances. She was a champion bridge player and competed with big shots, diplomats, movers and shakers. One of them, an ambassador, offered her a visa to Nicaragua; another said he could get her one to Scotland. Scotland was closer, so she took her son and daughter, *my* future half brother and sister, to an uncle and aunt in Belgium where they would be safe while she set up their new home across the Channel. It was a bad plan. The war escalated, borders were sealed, and my mother couldn't get back to her children. The only letters that were sent were by way of the Red Cross and I think my uncle and aunt didn't know what to say, so they said nothing. As a result, my mother thought her kids were okay. No news is good news. She didn't know my brother had been grabbed by the Nazis and taken to Auschwitz; she wouldn't know for three years. Miraculously, he survived.

My mother was, by training and talent, a much-in-demand couturier back in Vienna, but these were tough times and no one anywhere in Europe was having ball gowns made, so she took several demeaning jobs before getting one as a maid for really rich people who lived in a huge house. That was another bad plan—the real Queen Elizabeth would have had less "attitude." My mother liked the house, not the job. When the war ended she knew she needed to get permanent status in Great Britain so she could get her children back *and* stop cleaning toilets.

At a small local restaurant run by other displaced Europeans that served up schnitzel and anything with pork and potatoes, my mother met Greta, another vivacious Austrian and soon-to-be life-long best friend. I always thought she was my mother's real sister, the way they squabbled and read each other's minds. They quickly became a Euro version of Lucy and Ethel, and almost instantly hit upon their big plan: finding husbands. A nice Scottish woman who worked at the post office warned them, "All the good men are either dead or taken. It's only the old, broken, and illiterate ones that are still hanging about and no one wants them." Elizabeth and Greta smiled. They weren't fussy; it was British passports they were after.

They restricted their hunt down to dances and teas thrown by the hospitals or universities, which narrowed the prospects down to the crippled and the well-read. Greta scored on their first night out. She met Josef, a handsome Polish go-getter who had suffered a leg injury early in the war but had fought on the right side and managed to gain legal status. For them it was love. My mother continued to strike out but, on her fifth foray, the bells went off, the chimes chimed.

She saw him at a dance. He wasn't dancing. He was standing alone but he was, at least, standing. My Austro-Hungarian mother was a pistol, larger than life, vivacious and ferociously independent and my father-to-be was a musty, fifty-two-year-old virgin. My mother spotted the awkward Englishman standing next to the bar, examining one bottle after another, mumbling their identities, alcohol content, and whatever else it said, even in the fine print. He worked his way through the entire collection: "Drambuie 1867, I wouldn't mind a wee dram of that I'll tell you; Glenfiddich, single malt whiskey, oh yes, very nice, very nice indeed; Crème de Menthe, not bloody likely, I'd rather have a gurgle of Old Spice." When he was finished cataloging the liquor collection he switched his gaze and began reading whatever signage he could fixate on: "Pull in case of emergency. *Hmm* . . . I suppose that would mean in the event of a fire, or possibly an air raid. Not bloody likely, there'd be a stampede." Dick (his real name, honest) was perfect. My mother swooped in and scooped him right into her net. He never stood a chance. He went to the slaughter quickly and quietly. They were married ten days after they met.

It was his first and only time. She knocked back an entire bottle of Schnapps then handed him a bottle of iron pills and the sawdust flew. I guess she slept with him because Hallmark thank-you cards hadn't been invented yet.

"How could I be pregnant . . . from . . . from . . . that dry piece of old meat?"

Usually people are excited about having a baby. Not my mother. She was forty-four and was irritated by the very idea. I was a mistake. My father was the *real* mistake, but I existed as a constant reminder and I was not ever going to be something or someone who could be swept under the rug. She told me she had thought about throwing herself down the stairs but she somehow knew she'd just break her legs and still be pregnant with me. She didn't say it to be cruel, just as a statement of fact. I'm just guessing, but I don't think I was a love child.

My parents only did it once. My mother told me this often and every time she did, she'd shudder at the memory. "He was dry as dust." She was as layered as savory strudel and my very vivid imagination embarked on many a scenario, some involving thrusting tweed and upended dirndls, and worse. I am scarred by the notion: Dick lying on his back, glasses askew, the scent of mildew floating above him, with my mother straddling him in high black boots, her blonde helmet intact, a haze of Evening in Paris mingled with Aqua Net, her eyes squeezed closed. There was no way she was going to keep them open, but there was a smile on her face as she thought of that British passport to security.

Having achieved her goal, my mother showed my father the door before I was one month old and he returned quite happily to his prior life as a quiet, well-read boarder in a house that rented rooms to lonely gentlemen. My mother was determined to regain her position as dressmaker to the well-heeled, moving both her business and our home into a ludicrously large house in a prestigious neighborhood she could not afford but had to have, immediately immersing herself in swathing the ample bosoms of rich clients in beaded laces and linens.

My only constant companion was Sheila, our gruff housekeeper. I think she was about forty. She had little patience for my constant questions, but as we went on countless expeditions through every room of the hundred-year-old house—from the locked attic, through the large formal rooms, and down to the coal cellar in the basement—she relished in terrifying both of us with her constant narrative of the ghosts and axe-murderers who she believed once inhabited my new home. It was on those forays that my future dread of entering any empty house was born. From then on, all my arrivals were announced by me making a racket of some kind, as a warning to any ghosts or living intruders that they had better get out fast because I was armed and dangerous.

When my half sister and brother were finally reunited with my mother and came to live with us, I was almost incoherent with excitement. Somehow I was convinced they were going to become my playmates. So when I was first introduced to Gerda and Peter I was shocked that they were not children, but grownups.

Gerda was twenty-three and beautiful, and wanted nothing more than to move forward and erase all memories of the terrible war and what it had cost her. She threw herself into conquering all the eligible men in Glasgow and before long she was inundated with suitors.

My twenty-two-year-old Auschwitz survivor half brother was another story. He looked like a skinny hyena but still handsome, even though he had a disease in his lungs and needed to sleep a lot so he could get better. He wasn't really up for playing Daddy to me, but I anointed him with the job anyway, following him around like a lovesick puppy, sitting outside his room, waiting for him to wake up. When he would finally have breakfast, even if it was lunchtime, I would eat a second breakfast right next to him. Sheila would huff and puff about all the extra dishes she had to wash, but then she'd make sure Peter got fresh cream for the hot scones she would always make him. I had to sneak some when she wasn't looking. My mother kept telling me to leave him alone, explaining what a nightmare it was for him over there in that hell of a place, and that now what he needed was peace and quiet. She added, "You can't know how awful it was for him." I was quick to respond, "How could I not know, seeing as *everyone* tells me all the time?"

Peter had so many things he wanted to do and places he wanted to explore, but I glommed onto him like a mollusk he couldn't shake so he finally gave in and began taking me along. He craved being outside in big open spaces and all he wanted me to do was be quiet, which was nearly impossible as I had so many questions: Why was he so thin? What are Nazis? Why didn't he like being inside? Did he have nightmares when he slept during the daytime? I followed him around every golf course in Scotland, chattering away because I was so excited to have someone to talk to. I chattered his ear off as we hiked around hills and dales. Mostly, I sat on a hill waiting and picking heather while Peter hiked. He took me to Loch Ness and pointed out a big, dark shape that he said was a monster that lived in the lake to protect all of Scotland from Nazis and other bad people. I was in love.

My father had taken to visiting me every other Sunday unless my mother had other ideas for me, like the dreaded elocution classes she signed me up for to cure my sibilance—it didn't. He always arrived with a bag filled with hard candy and various vitamins for my growth. Could he be to blame for my ever-growing girth? We sat together sucking candy with me mimicking his breathing patterns just to fill the uncomfortable pauses between him reading the labels on the candy bags and on the bottles of kelp: "Brain food, can't get too much of that right?" Bee pollen: "Mark my words, excellent for arthritis, nasty business." I nodded. I was seven. I had no idea what arthritis was, but I knew I didn't want it. I took the pills.

Mummy and Greta were deep in cahoots with their next big plan: to find Peter a rich wife. I think my mother felt guilty and desperately wanted to make up for not being there to protect him, and to make sure that from now on he would have a safety net to fall back on. She zeroed in on one of the wealthy Austrians whom she knew had a single and not-yet-married daughter. Suzie was pretty but extremely heavy, and in Glasgow's closely knit Jewish community, there were few pickings. It was perfect. Neither my brother nor his intended had much say in the plan, but a wedding was soon enough in the works despite the fact that neither Peter, nor Suzie, seemed ready or enthralled by the prospect. However, both succumbed to the pressure of pushy parents.

I wasn't quite sure what was happening but I knew it wasn't good, especially when I had to stand still for endless pin-sticking fittings for a yellow bridesmaid dress that had skirt wings trimmed in black rick-rack. "Ouch!" Another pin stuck me as I tried to escape. "I look like a bumble bee. You should cancel the wedding, he doesn't love her."

My mother twirled me around and looked straight into my eyes with fierce determination. "Your brother is getting married and he's going to be happy and that's final."

Weddings were supposed to be happy and beautiful. This one didn't seem that way to me. Me and two other prettier bumble bees,

Suzie's cousins, followed the bride and groom down the aisle to tie the knot that seemed more like it was around their necks than anywhere else.

At the reception, I have a distinct memory of clinging to my brother's leg as he danced the first slow dance with "her." She tried to dislodge me, but I was not that easy to shake off and I was on a mission to make my brother see he was making a terrible mistake. He bent down and patted me on the head as he tried to pry me loose. "It's going to be okay, I will still take you to our special places."

I didn't believe him and I whispered, "Would you marry me if I was older? I can cook and I can iron and I can be charming. I can."

He pulled away as he twirled Suzie in the opposite direction but not before whispering back, "Yes you can." But he was gone.

I went directly toward the man cutting the wedding cake into uniform little slices and asked for two pieces.

2

Abominable

Diet #2 ✦ **Eat nothing that tastes good**

Cost ✦ **My ability to fly**

Weight lost ✦ **Not enough**

Weight gained ✦ **None**

My sister, after leaving half a dozen broken hearts in her wake, married Phil, a newly minted doctor, and there was rejoicing all through our large, unaffordable house. Along with the usual Austrians there were irascible Scots and a smattering of outrageous, loud Brits, but best of all there was apple strudel, Sacher tortes, Punschkrapfen, and all the whipped cream in the kingdom. I was in heaven, my fingers and mouth sticky with evidence. After the wedding, unlike Peter and Suzie, the happy couple left for "Dusseldorf . . . Dusseldorf . . . Dusseldorf," (how

I loved that word) Germany, where Phil was stationed and where he and Gerda would live for a year.

The giant house felt even bigger; it was definitely colder as my mother didn't have money to pay for a wedding *and* heat, but the party was far more important to feed her delusions of grandeur. Whenever I said I was cold, her response was to tell me to put on more sweaters and stop complaining as it was more important to live in a good neighborhood where there was opportunity to meet a better class of people. She was furious when I wondered, *What if all these people are pretending to be rich, too?*

When she wasn't working, which was hardly ever, my mother was plotting get-rich schemes with Greta or playing kill-or-be killed bridge games with her posse of temperamental blue-haired Viennese ex-pats, and their endless swirls of blue smoke curling upwards from their overflowing ashtrays. I would sit watching, mesmerized momentarily by the glass shelves filled with sterling silver candy dishes, fruit bowls, and silver bric-a-brac all engraved with her name on them for being the best bridge player in the world. I sat watching, waiting, and then willing the games to end, followed by gentle but malevolent chair-banging against the wall until my mother would either shoot me a death stare or suggest in no uncertain terms that I take a piece of cake and go to my room to enjoy it. It was hard to imagine that these so-called games brought on pleasure with all the shouting: "You are a cheat!" "You are a liar!" "*Accch*, I fold . . ." Inevitably came the volley of guttural native-tongue swearing, the sound of chairs scraping backward, coats put on, followed by the slamming of doors. Everyone was always leaving in a huff, yet they'd be back two nights later to engage in more warfare. I hated bridge.

I had always been a little pudgy, but when my mother had me try on whatever new itchy wool dress she was making for me, I could see frustration in her face followed by her favorite "*Aaacch . . .*" and then a seam would be ripped apart and re-pinned, this time looser. She never said a word but I knew. I believe I began my lifelong love affair with food to fill some hole, but also so that I would get bigger and bigger so that I couldn't be ignored. Food soon filled any void created by too much information and isolation, allowing my skin to thicken, along with all my other parts.

Despite my being as solid as a tree trunk, I desperately wanted to be a ballerina. I loved my ballet classes with Miss Bellshaw, the beautiful teacher who really looked like a long-necked swan and who told *me* before anyone else that we were going to have our first recital in a real theatre. I practiced every day at class and when I got home from school; at night I had dreams of myself in pink tulle, twirling and leaping in magnificent *grand jetés* across the stage to thunderous applause. But there are rules about what a fat person can and cannot do and I learned them at age seven in my premiere ballet performance.

Many of my classmates were scared and had trouble breathing normally, but when I stepped onto the stage and looked out at all the parents, uncles, and aunts sitting in the audience, I couldn't stop smiling—this was where I wanted to be. Dressed in identical tutus, we all held hands as we came out onto the stage and made a circle of fluttering feet and hands. Then we let go, and each of us twirled into the light and leapt as high as we could, which at our age was minimal. The goal was to have our *attempt* at greatness be appreciated, but what I got instead at my first public performance was a crescendo of ever-building murmurs of, "*Aaw*, how cute and so chubby! Watch her jump," followed by the sound of laughing. From that time on, all my dance performances were done behind closed doors in my bedroom.

Extreme caution and hypersensitivity to the lurking danger zones became second nature. No swim parties for me; I never wanted to give any of those splashing, happy, skinny, mean kids the opportunity to shout out, "Nessie!"—the common nickname for the Loch Ness Monica. At school I tried to walk in the center of the largest crowd, hoping to have it swallow me up; the danger was heightened if I was ahead of the pack, alone and out there asking for ridicule. I never, ever volunteered an answer in class, and I never ate in front of anyone because that would only have encouraged the smart-asses.

One truly humiliating moment of complete abandon came during an unusual snowstorm. Making my first-ever snow angel in the fresh powder, I lay on my back, exuberantly flapping my arms and legs. The sounds of happy kids pelting each other with snowballs must have desensitized my tuned-in, fat-attack meter, but suddenly, feeling all eyes upon me, the alarm bells rang. I got up and scurried away but not before hearing one of the older kids yell, "Abominable Snowman sighting! Look at that huge hole in the snow, there's the proof!" The others ran over to look at the crop circle made by an alien spaceship.

I was not yet strong enough to stand up to bullies so I ran home, the sound of their taunts still ringing in my ears. I was in desperate need of comfort, but everyone was busy so I found my comfort in other ways—food and dismemberment. I loved to take things apart. I had a giant doll almost the same height as I was and I was fond of operating on her, removing limbs to see how they were attached; I was never quite as good at putting them back. I loved to cut her hair and her clothes. My mother was not pleased. I turned a fallen-down, heavy window shutter into a stage and I took my old baby carriage apart and turned it into a go-cart and a rocker. I lured the neighborhood children to our back garden with promises of rides and a host of ever-changing plays, which only I would star in. I finally had the attention I had been craving. There was a backlash brewing, but I was too enamored with my position as ringmaster to notice until all of my newfound friends rebelled, calling me bossy, and then left.

My father continued his every-other Sunday visits and still we mostly spent that time together not getting to know each other. It was just something that we did and I accepted it as my normal. Out of boredom and loneliness I started to hang about my mother's workroom with all of her seamstresses. They had far more patience for my stream of questions than my mom. I wanted to know why the cloth-covered dress form was called a dummy and why it didn't have arms. It didn't make any sense. "People have arms, don't they? If they are having dresses made, they will need them to fit their arms and there's none there to make sure their sleeves will be okay." Estella, one of the seamstresses, gave me a pad of paper and drawing pencils and told me to draw some dresses. She probably did this to get me to shut up. My first drawing was a soft green, silk, long gown and had long pearls hanging all over the front. It turned out I could draw and Estella showed it to my mother who showed it to one of her clients, who really liked it and had my mother make it. It was not quite the same but close enough to be the dress from my drawing. It was the first time I remember feeling proud, but even better than that, I knew my mother was proud of me, too. I was eight.

My euphoria didn't last as my mother had signed me up for swimming lessons. Bathing suits and baring skin was already a sensitive issue but that wasn't to be my problem. It came in the form of the instructor who was really old and really mean, with wrinkly brownish skin from being in the sun too much. I don't think he liked children. There were eight of us and Mr. Simpson treated us all equally—he yelled at every one of us. He bellowed nonstop: "Pay attention! Face in, bubbles out, left arm in, right arm out, breathe, kick, breathe, kick . . . " I still didn't understand which came first and I always swallowed a lot of water. To make matters even worse, the black lake was freezing cold. At least we wore cork belts to help keep us afloat. Mine, unfortunately, was too tight but I didn't dare say anything because I didn't want to be singled out.

We were all scared of him but, after two weeks of swimming about in the frigid lake, at last I began to feel more secure—then Mr. Simpson told us the belts were coming off and we were going to swim away from the dock to the deep part of the lake. I wasn't at all ready for this step! I was terrified and told him I couldn't do it. He spun around and shouted, "Yes, you can!"

"I can't!" I whimpered.

He barked over and over, "Yes, you can!"

I tried to walk away but he came and got me and stared into my eyes, saying, "Get in the water or you won't be given your swimming certificate."

I started to cry. "I'm afraid. . . ."

Then, out of nowhere, Peter appeared and told Mr. Simpson that I didn't have to do it because he was taking me sailing. My brother had saved me just like some handsome prince in a fairy tale.

As we headed out into the lake, the water was a little choppy and I felt a little bit seasick but I knew it would go away because I was so happy and that feeling was bigger than any other. We were way out in the middle of the lake when Peter dropped the anchor. The wind was calmer now and we played a game of twenty questions. I won. Peter stood up, looking out onto the water. "Come see," he said. I did but I didn't know what I was supposed to be looking for when I felt a hand on my back and he pushed me. I fell overboard and into the deep water. I felt myself sinking, going below the surface. *Glub, glub, glub.* I popped back up, gasping for air.

Peter shouted at me to swim to the boat. "Kick your legs. You can do it!" I saw him leaning forward, his arm outstretched. I kicked and paddled and moved toward him. He hauled me up and back into the boat. "See, you can swim; you just think too much about what you can't do. It gets in the way. Sometimes you have to just *do*, that's how you survive." We headed back for the shore and for a while we didn't speak. There was just the sound of the sails flapping against the wind. I was still shocked that I knew how to swim and I thought about what Peter had said. I somehow knew he wasn't just talking about me.

3

A Fresh Start

Diet #3 ✦ **All the Empress's Cakes**

Cost ✦ **My mother's hat and what little trust I ever had**

Weight lost ✦ **None**

Weight gained ✦ **Five pounds and counting**

I came home from school late one afternoon and found the front lawn filled with giant cardboard boxes; three of them were labeled: "Monica's room." The front door was wide open, and when I went in I was horrified to see that all our furniture was gone! I ran up the stairs to my room and it was completely empty. So was my mother's room. I ran down the back stairs and banged into a lumbering hulk of a man in a brown uniform carrying one of my mother's sewing machine tables. "What's happening? Why are you taking that?" He just kept moving like a steam engine and I was scared, but those were our things, not his, so I gripped the bannister and looked up at him straight in his eyes. He saw I had no intention of stepping aside until he answered me, and I was costing him precious time. He blew outward, "I canny answer ya' much Hen but I can tell ya' it's all going in the truck down to Greenock." What was Greenock? Where was my mother? I ran back up the stairs and then down through every empty room until I found her in a back hallway closet, zipping up a heavy canvas bag filled with coats: her Persian, my duffel, and my brand-new shocking pink wool coat. She had a big red marking pen in her hand and on the bag she was writing "SHIP."

I asked, "Mummy, what's happening?"

She responded, "We are going to have a wonderful new life." I liked my old life; nobody bothered with me and I did whatever I wanted. But we were moving—to Canada! My mother missed my sister, as it had been two years since we had seen her and Phil, and now they had a baby! Add that to all the time she didn't have with her because of the war and now she was also a grandmother, so she was determined to make up for lost time. But I thought the real reason was because she was lonely. Her sidekick, Greta, had also moved to Canada with her husband and their son, who was just a few months older than I was. He was my pretend cousin, just like Greta was my pretend aunt. Whatever the reason, it was happening and we were moving. Suddenly I felt sick. I would be going to a new school. I was fat and now there would be new people to make fun of me. Overwhelmed and scared, I carried a whole pile of my baby toys, including the big doll on whom I had performed so many surgeries that she looked like the pictures from newsreels of wounded girls who somehow survived the war. I was dumping them all into a big garbage bin when I noticed a framed photograph sticking out from under a pile of rubbish. It was my mother and father's wedding photo: a black-and-white picture of both of them all dressed up, holding hands because of the occasion but staring straight out, looking like strangers. I came to understand much later that nothing was that black and white. I took it out of the frame and folded it. I still have it. The crease down the middle separating them says so much.

An order of nuns bought our big house and were planning on turning it into a convent. I wondered if they knew my mother was Jewish. I was not sure what I was because my father belonged to the United Church of England, which made no sense to me because from everything I learned in school, the churches in England had never been united.

Everything we owned was piled high and loaded in the big moving truck. We were getting ready to leave when my father made an unannounced visit. He had heard about her plan and he was livid. I had never ever seen him like that, and I felt oddly proud when he blocked my mother's path, "You will not take my daughter out of this country. I have rights and you mark my words she's not going to any bloody damn Canada!" My mother was in a state of disbelief, she had no idea my father had it in him to raise his voice or to make any demands of her. He'd found his balls.

She could barely find her voice, and was somehow unable to direct any of it at him, so she said what she wanted to say to me, "Can you believe it? The mealworm suddenly grew a spine. Rights? *Aaacchh. . . .*" She hopped around stymied for a moment until she recovered her aplomb and could face him. "I apologize for . . . well, for . . . none of that matters. I think we should start over and we'll be a family." She took a breath. She knew that was exactly what he wanted. I had never lived with a mother and a father. I was excited because we'd be normal.

We took a huge ship to Canada called *The Empress of Scotland*. My mother and I shared a stateroom with a small porthole that looked out over a never-ending sea of huge black waves. My father had his own room and I guessed they were not starting their "new start" until we got there. We had been at sea for five days and all the grownups were seasick; there was a hurricane off the coast of Labrador turning the waves into giant mountains that made the ship go up really high on one end and then smash down onto the other, over and over, so that the swimming pool kept emptying and then filling up again but with less water each time. No one was allowed in the pool.

I had made a new best friend named Hannah and we were the only two left who could walk around. She was from Montreal and she was tall and skinny and wore a bra. I wished I looked like her but I didn't; I was flat and fat, but together we were a "10." Hannah was wild and supremely confident, unlike me, and she dragged me into the nearly empty, big, beautiful ballroom that had tables laden with amazing cakes, desserts, and piles of crystal bowls to fill with whatever one wanted. The sailors and even the captain danced with Hannah. I sat watching as she was twirled around and around, her head thrown back in total euphoria. I filled a plate with a sponge cake, fruit, and whipped cream trifle. It was delicious and distracted me from the unfairness—I was a good dancer, too! Just then our eyes met and I waved, pretending to be happy, and then Hannah pulled me up to dance. I loved her.

We dressed up every night as if we were movie stars with servants and no one ever said we had eaten enough sweets or fizzy drinks or that it was time for us to go to bed. One night, Hannah and I climbed into a lifeboat and I brought a whole chocolate cake that I asked for and got; Hannah brought wine. We told each other everything, all our secrets, promising we would be best friends forever and together we wished that our magical voyage would never end.

Feeling more than a little bit tipsy, we climbed out of our hiding place and Hannah pushed me in the direction of the empty bar, somehow knowing the staff was bored with no one to serve and that they would be only too happy to be entertained by a pair of twelve-year-olds. I was nervous about going into the forbidden bar, and to stall I insisted we stop by my cabin first and get hats from my mother's hatboxes in order to pass as more mature.

Pumped and primped, we brazenly stepped into the bar. I was wearing a chinchilla hat with feathers while Hannah wore a red, large-brimmed one with black ostrich feathers and matching lipstick. When we climbed onto the leather barstools I felt instantly more sophisticated. The bartenders mixed up frothy pink, nonalcoholic drinks with umbrellas in them, then switched to green ones with pineapple spears and maraschino cherries. We were enthralled by their stories of the parties passengers had on the high seas, but those were no match for what the crew got up to when everyone else was sleeping or throwing up on the rough crossings.

After an hour or so, with still no appearances from any of the passengers, the bartenders, Paolo and Reuben, our new friends, told us to follow them to the main deck where they rolled out four luggage carts with fast-moving metal wheels. We all lay on our stomachs, kicking off with our feet as we raced each other, careening all over the highly varnished wood deck, laughing crazily, banging into railings and into each other like bumper cars. It all came to a sudden stop when one of the more stern-faced officers stepped out of a stairwell and glared at all of us but mostly at Paolo and Reuben.

It was our last night, as we were to land in Quebec City the next day and I was going on to Toronto by train. For the first time on our voyage, the boat stopped rocking against the high waves. Everything had suddenly become very calm; the water was black and shiny and very still, and a million stars appeared as if orchestrated. We heard doors opening as the passengers, feeling better, began to arrive on the deck in droves, but the captain invited *us* to go up on the bridge. "Watch the horizon, lassies." A great mountain of blue white ice appeared out of nowhere, then another and another—icebergs! They were the mountains of the sea.

It was awe-inspiring but all of a sudden I felt strange as if my stomach flip-flopped and then turned upside down, and I felt my mouth tighten. The captain noticed my discomfort, "You don't have to be scared Lassie, I never get over the sight of them." Suddenly there was a deep, deep low rumbling sound and I was sure we had hit one and that we were going to sink. *"Oh God!"* I threw up all over the captain's shiny black shoes; Hannah looked at me and I could see her move away from me. She was embarrassed. A steward began wiping the deck; another put a blanket around me and led me away.

When I woke up in our cabin it was morning and weirdly quiet, but my head was throbbing. The engines had stopped and I relished the silence, but then I realized my mother and all our bags were gone. We were here, in Canada! The decks were jammed with people and porters running in every direction. I had to find Hannah, we hadn't said good-bye and I didn't have her address. I saw my mother and father leaning over the railing searching for my sister Gerda and her husband Phil. I confronted my mother about leaving me in the cabin even though we had landed. She shook her head impatiently, explaining she didn't want to miss a good viewing spot and it wasn't as if I could get lost on a boat. I had stopped listening when I saw Hannah and her parents walking down the gangway. I shouted her name but she didn't hear me. Panicking, I bellowed her name at the top of my lungs; "HANNAH!" She still didn't hear me and then I realized, she didn't want to hear me. But she was my best friend! Oh my God! She was wearing my mother's red hat, its ostrich plume swaying as she walked.

My mother started waving like a maniac. She had found my sister, her husband, and their baby, and then I saw them, too. They were searching for us, too, and I waved and jumped up and down in excitement as my beautiful (thin) half sister found us. She nudged Phil hard in his ribs when she saw my father and I realized my mother hadn't told them he was coming. But then Gerda saw *me*. Her mouth opened as if making a horror movie scream. We hadn't seen them in nearly two years and I was a little heavier. I hated them, and I knew I was going to hate Canada, too.

4

Firsts

Diets #4 & #5 ✦ **Dexedrine & Metrecal**

Cost ✦ **$62.00**

Weight lost ✦ **15 pounds**

Weight gained ✦ **22 pounds**

It was hot and sticky and hard to breathe, and there were giant spiders that bite, and black flies that bite, and teeny mosquitoes that bite, and they could all see in the dark. We were living with Gerda, her husband, and their screaming baby who had a chronically runny nose. I was his aunty, but even worse, I had to share a room with him. At night when he'd cry, no one came because they knew I was there to pick him up. What I really wanted to do was put a pillow over his snot-nosed face.

Canada was weird. Everything was new; even the trees outside my sister's house were the same height as I was and everywhere we went there were these boring shopping plazas, whereas in Scotland all the shops were jumbled together on busy main streets. My dad was having a really hard time, having no idea what he was supposed to do, who he was supposed to be, or how to fit in. And nobody paid any attention to him. I felt bad but we didn't really know how to talk to each other either.

One day we were having a special dinner for all the family and friends to welcome us to Canada. The table was already set and it was only seven in the morning! My sister was already running around fluffing and picking up lint that wasn't there, straightening cushions and wiping up spots that didn't exist, when she stopped to give me a long, appraising look. "You should watch what you eat and then you'll lose weight." It really bothered her that I was overweight. Well, it really bothered me, too, but I wanted to tell her to shut up and mind her own business.

The chairs soon filled with new relatives who were old and neighbors who kept wanting me to talk so they could try and mimic my accent—badly, I might add—and they all had opinions on everything. Everyone was loud and had stories to tell and there was tons of food, but my plate had hardly anything on it because I could feel I was being watched. I pretended to go to the bathroom but instead I slipped into the kitchen and started shoveling potatoes, brisket, and everything else into my mouth. Then I heard them coming—all the women, carrying plates, and then scraping the leftovers into the sink. I swallowed without chewing and gave them a guilty wave.

Suddenly, the house started shaking and everyone looked out the window to see if it was thundering. There wasn't a cloud in the sky; instead, the whirling vortex of energy was my sister, in her bedroom, furiously pedaling on her Exercycle and sending shockwaves through the house. "I'm just burning off what I've eaten," she said, patting little beads of sweat from her chest.

Looking me up and down, I could see her making mental calculations of every fat cell in my body. "Phil knows a doctor who would prescribe diet pills for you that would do the trick," she said breathlessly. "You might start smoking . . . but you wouldn't have an appetite, so it'd be worth it." I reminded her I was only twelve.

She made me an appointment with my first diet doctor. I didn't want to go to a "fat" doctor but my sister convinced my mother that my very future was at stake if I didn't lose weight. My mother interpreted that to mean no one would ever marry me, so here we were, sitting in a room full of fat people all waiting for their miracle.

The doctor was old and stick thin. He looked me over and then pointed his finger in my face. He was very angry with me. I wanted to kick him. I tried to make eye contact with my mother but she was fixated on everything in that little office except me. The doctor began his tirade. "You are too young to be so fat! I can help you but only if you promise to take these special pills I am going to give you. Do you understand?" I nodded in agreement so we could get out of there. I was afraid I would cry and I didn't want him to know how upset I was. The pills were little black-and-white tubes called Dexedrine. As he walked us out and back to the waiting room to greet his next victim, he dismissed me: "Take the pills at breakfast, lunch, and dinner." I scurried away as fast as I could get me and my mother out of there.

What Doctor Meanie really meant with his stupid pills was that I wouldn't *need* breakfast, lunch, *or* dinner. I was jittery and cranky all the time. I had no appetite and I was unable to fall asleep. I didn't like them, so then I pretended to take them but I flushed them down the toilet instead. That meant I was hungry nearly all the time. I hid chocolate bars in the back of the freezer, wrapping them in foil as if they were leftovers.

Soon my own personal Gestapo, my sister, found them and confronted me, "Look at me. This figure takes work. It doesn't just happen; it takes discipline. I am trying to save you from yourself." I had gone from having a mother who didn't care what I was doing to having a maniac sister and brother-in-law who followed me around as if they were food police. The evidence of my transgression was laid out on the kitchen table to rub my face in it. I was humiliated and angry that it bothered them that I was fat. Yet for some weird reason that I didn't understand, it also made me happy. I quickly understood my size gave me power and, with that knowledge, I began to carve out my identity. I told my sister that I already had a mother and she should butt out of my life.

After a few long months, we moved to a place of our own—my mother, my father, and I. Was this to be the beginning of their new start? It wasn't going as well as I had hoped, the first hint being the horrifying knowledge that we were poor. Having come from a huge, drafty Scottish house (now home to a whole nest of nuns) we were now huddled in a shockingly small two-bedroom apartment—all three of us! My father was in one bedroom and my mother and I hunkered down in the other. I guessed they were never really going to be like other married couples. My mother had found the apartment she had to have, almost in Forest Hill, the richest neighborhood she could find, where everyone was snobby and dressed exactly the same. It was like living right next door to a bakery, with the mouthwatering scent of chocolate éclairs wafting out the door from dawn until dusk, but never having enough money to actually have one.

The kids at my new school looked at me as if I was from Jupiter. Not only was I poor, but I was also fat and had an accent—a troika of undesirableness. The popular kids rejected me instantly, but I found my soul mates. The misfits, artists, and outsiders were waiting for me with open arms. I couldn't have asked for a better fit. Being disallowed united us, and being different became our art form.

Up until now, my mother had always worked at home, but here in Canada, in order to elevate her profile and attract business, she signed a lease on a shop in the very upscale Yorkville neighborhood. This was a big risk and added to her financial burden. My father once again undersold himself and got a job at the University of Toronto as a caretaker. I was mortified, but because he was English, "tweedy," and very smart, I pretended he was a professor. I was definitely my mother's daughter in the delusions of grandeur business.

My parents always got home late from work and I hated arriving home to an empty apartment. I stood outside every afternoon and steeled myself against my own spiraling imagination. With every rustle of the leaves or settling of the foundation, I conjured up images of serial killers lying in wait, or burglars in the bushes casing the joint. I climbed the stairs and before opening my door, I'd shout in my most manly and scary voice, "You have three minutes to get out!" Then I would fling the door open to crush whoever might still have the audacity to be lingering, pick up the phone to make sure the wires hadn't been cut, pull a steak knife from the drawer, and finally do a thorough check under the beds and in the closets. Once I was sure our home was free of intruders, I would relax and load up on cake and chocolate ice cream. We always had cake—my mother was, after all, Viennese.

After school everyone else went to hang out at either some very cool ice cream shop I would never see, or one of their enormous houses, to try on each other's clothes. I was glad I wasn't invited—I would never have fit into any of those crappy designer clothes anyway. Instead, I had a job three days a week after school and on Saturdays at my Uncle Carly and Aunty Mara's delicatessen, slicing meat and packaging it to give to a lot of garlicky smelling old people.

This wasn't right. This couldn't be my life. I had read about Anastasia, the missing daughter of the Tsar and Tsarina of Russia, and I prayed every night that someone from the Russian royal family would realize I was their Anastasia and come and rescue me. The fact that she was alive decades before my birth didn't phase me. No one ever came, and I sliced meat for two years.

My mother couldn't stand her brother Carly; she had tried to spend most of her life not speaking to him. My family could have created a board game about who was not speaking to whom. Someone was always on the outs with someone and I'm pretty sure my mother was one of those someones. Carly had a history of making bad business deals and sketchy investments with other people's money, and more than once he scorched my mother when she bought into whatever nonsense he was peddling. He was good at selling and he lost not only her hard-earned money but Greta's as well.

Carly reminded me of a boiled potato who had married another boiled potato, shapeless and without definition to their features. He appeared stupid but he wasn't; he was as canny as a fox. He wore *lederhosen* and his wife Mara wore dirndls and they both dyed their hair Russian salad-dressing blonde, making them look like a matching pair of scary cuckoo-clock inhabitants.

I think my mother's fury toward him really came when he happened to buy a delicatessen in Toronto's financial district and it unexpectedly became a gold mine, with a daily lineup of customers that was almost as long as the line of relatives all wanting their money back from his previous bad investments. In truth, she was jealous. Carly made promises to repay her in a few months when he was sure he was on solid ground. My mother wasn't falling for anything he said; she had heard his promises and lies too often and she wanted her pound of flesh and then some, and she was willing to take it in bratwurst, schinken, Hungarian salami, pickles, or sauerkraut. It was my job to sneak it out of there and bring home the bacon—literally. Mara was hawk-eyed, mean, and suspicious. She stood watch over the ham-slicer in case I had any ideas of stuffing myself with their profits. They watched me from dawn to dusk, hoping to catch me in the act, but they never did. I was only allowed to eat the things that didn't sell; stinky headcheese (what the hell was that?) and shaky things that were coved in aspic (what the hell was that?). I'd go next door to the bakery and load up on cherry cheese Danish and donuts just to get the taste out of my mouth.

But they made a terrible mistake when they falsely accused me of stealing from the till. Mara, a former Soviet with supposed connections to the much-feared KGB, confronted me as I came out of the bathroom. She bored into me with her piggy eyes and demanded I empty my pockets and lift my blouse. "I know you have taken our money and you have meat hidden on you. I can smell it."

I could not contain my unexpected burst of laughter. "This whole place stinks of meat." I turned my pockets inside out and lifted my blouse. There was nothing there. "I quit!" I exclaimed. With my head held high, I marched out and called my mother.

That was it! My mother and Carly had a face-off outside the delicatessen. They might as well have taken over Caesar's Palace and shown it on satellite. Everyone knew about it. Carly, looking like a rabid puffer fish, screamed in full-volume righteous indignation. My mother chose the more powerful stone-faced defense and very softly said, "You are dead to me. That is my *daughter* you are accusing—your own niece—and you, a man who has absconded twice with *my* money! You don't exist." With that, we turned and walked away. As soon as we were around the corner, I reached into my waistband and pulled out a pound and a half of Black Forest ham.

My mother waved her black-magic wand, and in a nanosecond she set the whole family against him. By the time she was done, he and Mara were toast—not invited to anything, not even a bris. It took a moment to register, but that was my mother defending me! The best part was, I no longer had to slice and serve sausage to garlicky old people.

We didn't see either of them again until Mara's funeral a year later. She died at the hair salon from a sudden heart attack, wearing a full head of perm rods. I always wondered if they combed her hair out before the big send off.

I thought things were beginning to look up. I had friends and my parents seemed to be getting along. A strange calm had settled over our apartment until my mother, standing at the bus stop once too often after seeing all her neighbors pulling in and out of their garages, went on a rampage, insisting that we needed a car. It was all she could talk about at every opportunity. This was the New World and everyone had a car except us. My father pointed out that it was all well and good to want a car but none of us knew how to drive one. I thought he had a valid point but that concept sent her into a tailspin, "You see how he thinks, from his big toe, not his head. You'll learn; you'll get a driving teacher."

My father got behind the wheel of his driving instructor's car only once. It occurred to me that perhaps he did *everything* only once. He spent four hours practicing gear changing, going from park to drive, and back to park, over and over until the almost comatose instructor insisted he put it into drive and take it for a spin. My mother and I stood in the supermarket parking lot watching in horror as the little blue car began jerking forward, heading directly toward a runaway shopping cart. My father honked and honked, but the cart didn't understand honking, and it smacked head-on into the car with a loud bang! Outraged, my father slammed on the brakes, got out of the car, and walked away, his clenched demeanor making it abundantly clear that his driving days were done.

I thought my mother was going to implode, "Dick, come back here, you have to learn to drive! *Aacch!* You see, you can't teach a dead dog new tricks." Two girls from my school were staring at her, then at me, and I heard them laughing. I could feel the fury building along with the hurt, but I pretended I didn't hear them. I knew that I'd be knocking back some really large and sugary dynamite as soon as I got home.

I wanted to lose weight but I couldn't seem to stop eating. What seemed more possible was losing my accent. I practiced relentlessly on storekeepers and strangers until I mastered sounding like a native, generic North American. But my parents' new start was crumbling rapidly. My father lost his job through no fault of his own. His position was eliminated by a cleaning service. He was home all the time and at loose ends, not quite sure how to move forward. My mother huffed and puffed at the mere sight of my father doing what he had always done, reading from the labels on everything. "Robertson's Marmalade . . . rather nice, made from sweet navel oranges; Morton's Iodized Salt . . . that is good. We do need iodine. . . ."

He took small pleasure in turning himself into an impenetrable block of stone whenever she directed any of her frustrations at him, which just made her seem more like a crazed Rumpelstiltskin. I could always tell when my mother was about to blow; she rode her vacuum cleaner hard into every nook and cranny, vitriol spewing from her in a stream of consciousness series of rants, as if it was the vacuum's exhaust. "*Aach*, mildew, that's what he smells of, old books, old wood, dust, death . . . keeping all his food in little piles in the fridge like a squirrel. I live with a squirrel, storing nuts for the winter. This is a country of supermarkets, with music and a thousand cereals!"

So is this what it was to be normal, to have a "real" family? Why did people want this so badly? It was a relief when it all came to an end and my father moved out, going back to his far simpler life. He was much happier going for strolls through Edwards Gardens in a park that reminded him of his beloved England. He always carried a camera but he never put film in it. It was a prop, to be used as a conversation starter as he posed the spinster postmistress from down the road in front of a bank of hydrangeas, or any one of the widows who rode on the same bus to the gardens. He was quite content between those outings and coming to visit me on Sundays, just as he always had, bringing candy and vitamins and being together, comfortably not talking. My mother had gathered a new tribe of blue-hairs that were as committed as she was to their biweekly battle of the bridge player, death-to-the-loser games.

I began to make friends. One of them, Vally, lived in the same building we did and she didn't have all the latest clothes either, but she had something better: big boobs, and a trail of cute boys who liked them. Vally was sweet and generous, and she took the boys, one at a time, down to the locker rooms where the suitcases and odds and ends of unused furniture were stored. Locker 308B was never locked and inside there was an ugly old, forgotten green couch where she let the boys touch her pride and joys.

I hung around outside, entertaining those waiting their turn with a running commentary on how each boy might be doing: "It's

Mark's turn at bat and it's possible he's going to get a home run." It never occurred to any of those boys to want to feel me up except for Rodney Sarner, who was nice, but short and pimply. One afternoon he took my hand and held it, his face moving in close to mine. Oh God, I knew he was going to kiss me, but I didn't know how to kiss so I scrunched my eyes closed until I felt his breath close to mine. I opened my eyes for a second and saw that his eyes were so close I could only see one of them, and it was smack in the center of his forehead. I panicked and stuck my tongue out at him. He let go of my hand and looked at me as if I were a freak. In fact, I was a freak. Vally told me later that she'd show me how to kiss. It felt so nice, safe, and not scary. Now I had another worry: "Oh God, I'm a lesbian."

I was practically sixteen and, despite my fears, it seemed I did like boys—specifically one boy. I was truly, madly, in love with Howie Bennett. Howie had dark and brooding good looks. He was smart, popular, and way out of my league, yet he was always kind and smiled in greeting as we passed in the hallway and I was smitten. He had absolutely no interest in me, but I wrote his name next to mine in every possible combination that would join us together even if it was only on paper. I cheered him on from the sidelines at track meets, even ogling him while he played street hockey. His friends began to tease him about me, but it was as if I was possessed. I dialed his phone number relentlessly; once, I was in such a dream state, I forgot to hang up. "Hello? Monica, I know it's you. . . ." I slammed the phone down and I can still remember the flop-sweat on my palms, my heart flip-flopping like a dying goldfish, and that feeling of total mortification—but I couldn't stop.

I resolved to go on my first real diet. I looked at every book on diets; there weren't many. The Drinking Man's Diet suggested drinking a cup of safflower oil to coat the stomach and then you could drink all the alcohol you wanted; I didn't want any. The Buttermilk Diet sounded yucky; I didn't like buttermilk. There was a new diet drink called Metrecal and it sounded perfect for me; it came in chocolate and strawberry. If I skipped breakfast and lunch and drank a tin of Metrecal instead, they promised I would lose weight. It tasted like chalk but the pounds seemed to fly off. I was willing to sacrifice flavor and the satisfaction of real food in order to have Howie see the real me hidden underneath the fat. Howie didn't know it yet but he was perfect for me, I just needed to figure out how to get him to see that.

On my sixteenth birthday, my mother gave me a surprise: a huge, yellow convertible. I immediately felt anxious. Other kids might have been thrilled at the prospect of receiving a car for their birthday but I knew my mother; she always had an ulterior motive. I might have had the keys to the car, but I was to be at her beck and call—her personal chauffeur, on duty seemingly every waking hour that I was not in school. I was expected to drive her, and sometimes all her other pink- and blue-haired friends to their bridge games, the delicatessen, the bakery, the hairdresser. Mostly, I wanted to drive them all right off a cliff. But I needed that car. Now that I had wheels, I had the ability to check up on Howie. Checking up is probably a tad understated; in reality, I became an obsessive stalker. I drove by his house over and over, hoping to get a glimpse of him or just to breathe the same air he was breathing. One day, I drove by and I saw his door open. I panicked and threw myself face down onto the empty passenger seat, knowing he was watching a very familiar giant yellow convertible driving by with *no* driver.

Even after that horror show, I couldn't stop. I was the hunter and he was my prey. I tailed him relentlessly. I knew Howie liked to play hockey so I put on my new white fuzzy hat and matching scarf over a pale pink, even fuzzier, sweater. In retrospect, I must have looked like a fat, cartoon character rabbit. To complete the look, I slung a pair of ice skates over my shoulder. I didn't skate and, honestly, the idea that anyone could glide, spin, or leap on those skinny little metal blades was beyond this big-assed girl's comprehension—but Howie didn't know that, and I had no plans to *ever* get on the ice so he would never find out.

I casually circled the rink about eighty times until he finally looked up. By that time I was hot and uncomfortable, but I smiled and waved, possibly a bit too exuberantly. Distracted by the sight of me, Howie whacked the puck so hard that it flew out of the rink, hitting my skates, which flew up in the air. One of the boots came down blade first, slicing through my hat, my hair, and finally my scalp. Blood gushed out from under my white fuzzy hat and I could feel myself getting dizzy but I knew I had to seize the moment: "Hi Howie."

His face twisted in a weird way and I was sure he hated me but gradually I understood—blood was dripping into my mouth and a big blotch landed on my white scarf. "Oh my God!" I felt faint but was determined not to let him see me pass out. "I have . . . a . . . a . . . I have to go. Great seeing you. Bye."

Twenty-seven stitches later, my non-relationship came to a horrible and even more humiliating end. How was that even possible?
I was at home with a bandage on my head and a bowl of ice cream
in my lap when the phone rang. It was Howie asking me if I was
busy on Friday night! I was stunned almost into silence. I couldn't
breathe. There really was some angel who went around and answered
prayers. "Um . . . I'm . . . I'm not busy," I said, my heart beating out
of my chest, "Um . . . what do you want to do? Whatever you want
would be whatever I would want to do, too."

I heard him swallowing hard, then came a long silence. I didn't
know what to say and it seemed, neither did he, but then he blurted
out that my mother had found his number on the cover of all of my
notebooks. *Oh God, oh God, no!* I thought to myself. He continued,
"She thought we had a thing, so she called me to ask me to take
you to your surprise birthday party on Friday at The House of
Chan and I didn't know what to say to that, and also I didn't want
to be rude, so . . ."

I couldn't feel my heart beating anymore, it must have stopped
when it got caught in my throat, and I was sure I was flat-lin-
ing. "What! Wait, my mother called you? My mother called you!
Oh . . . oh . . . *aaah* . . . Thank you, um, bye." I hung up and I sat
paralyzed, completely numb except for the extreme pounding in my
head, which wasn't coming from my stitches.

Shaking it off, I charged into the living room where, of course,
my mother was playing bridge with *the girls*. "You ruined my life!"
I screamed.

She didn't understand what she had done wrong but I knew she heard two and a half cases of Metrecal hitting the bottom of the metal garbage can, then the fridge door slamming after I grabbed a full quart of Neapolitan ice cream, followed by the banging of my bedroom door behind me.

5

Puppy Fat

Diet #6 ✦ **The Stillman Diet**

Cost ✦ **My pride**

Weight lost ✦ **12 pounds**

Weight gained ✦ **16 pounds**

I was eighteen and scarfing ham, chicken, beef strips, and every other type of former farm animal, all cooked with no oil, no sauce, and no taste because a Dr. Irwin Stillman had a new diet book that was all the rage, filled with promises of a leaner body just from eating a couple of hay-wagons worth of rump roasts. The monotonous chowing down on nothing but meat bored me stupid. Nonetheless, I gnawed like a zealot on those beef bones because everyone I knew except me had someone, and I needed to change that channel.

Every weekend my mother was off playing tournament bridge or being a better grandmother than an actual mother. She meant well, but she simply didn't have the Betty Crocker/Donna Reed gene. Seeing as I didn't date, she didn't think she had anything to worry about on the home front; she just figured I'd be hanging out with my other sad-sack girlfriends, inhaling pizza and ice cream. It no longer really mattered to me whether she was home or not; her absences meant I had the apartment to myself and I became notorious for my weekend open houses, as everyone knew my apartment was an adult-free zone. Cars lined my street, unloading hordes of young people, mostly kids I didn't know, and when the neighbors complained to my mother about the noise, she blew off the criticism by responding, "Call me if it ever gets quiet, then I'll know they're up to no good." She was actually thrilled to hear I was popular.

Being up to no good was, and still is, a teenage art form and my peers and I had it down to a science. To compensate for my lack of romance, I became a very skilled ringmaster of all things social, including orchestrating pizza deliveries and getting other people to pay for them. My newly discovered talent for matchmaking evolved into figuring out how long my mother's bedroom could be used for Seven Minutes in Heaven-style games. I didn't know it but I was exhibiting all the skills required to become a successful madam.

After the parties ended and I was left to pick up the detritus, the phone always rang with more than one of my friends, male and female, calling to get my guidance on whatever romantic entanglement was at hand. I was everyone's go-to girl for love advice and I was really good at it, which was ridiculous seeing as I'd never even had a boyfriend, just lots and lots of boy *friends*. Didn't they know I was making this stuff up?

Having given my singledom a lot of thought, I decided that losing my virginity was the key to becoming a woman. All my puppy fat would melt away and return to the puppy from whence it came and I would be desirable. With no one I could trust with my big plan, and therefore no one to warn me that this was a really bone-headed idea, I forged ahead and called my best guy pal Ben. I asked him if he wanted to hang out with some friends since there was no way I was going to give him any clues as to my agenda in case he freaked out and refused. Next I called Vally, who was "honored and excited to be part of my sexual awakening." I felt myself cringe when she said that out loud, but the plan was on. Vally was always up for an adventure, especially if it had to do with boys and sex. I, however, was scared to death.

But I did know there was no way anyone could get close to doing "it" with me while I was wearing my iron underwear; I was locked up tighter than a woman on death row. I unshackled myself from my long-line bra, prayed for the Jaws of Life to help release me from my triple-elasticized panty girdle, and I was open for business.

We were parked above a skating rink on the edge of a bluff also known as "Makeout Mountain: Over 1 billion served"; I desperately hoped to join in the tradition. Vally was in the front seat breathing heavily with some new guy called Barry, and I was in the back with Ben, who was already weirded out that we were on a double date and were now parked at the notorious Makeout Mountain.

Between the heavy breathing coming from the front seat and the dead silence coming from the back, I was embarrassed with the realization that this was not going as I had envisioned, but I had a mission to accomplish even if it was weird. I needed this to happen and I awkwardly offered myself up to Ben, who looked at me as if I had just undergone a head transplant. I made it even worse when I reached for his hand and timidly put it on my breast. He pulled it away as if he was Clark Kent and my boobs were Kryptonite and whispered, "Are you insane?" I stammered that we could just close our eyes and be quick about it and no one would ever have to know. Ben looked at me and laughed nervously and said we were friends and he wasn't attracted to me that way.

I told him that unless we *did it*, we wouldn't be friends in any way. I felt sick but this had to get done. When I suggested I could put my coat over my head and he could pretend I was Donna, one of my gorgeous girlfriends whom I knew he *really* liked, his whip-fast retort was that I could put ten coats over my head and he'd still know it was me because I never shut my mouth! I was mortified. I didn't even like Ben that way but I still felt hurt so I punched him hard in his ribs. I think he might have been about to twist my arm but just then the car began bouncing rhythmically as Vally and Barry reached some loud Nirvana-like state.

Could this get any worse? Apparently, yes. Vally, in the throes of ecstasy, threw a leg into the air and kicked the gearshift into drive; there was a grinding noise followed by a sudden lurch and the car was moving toward the precipice. Panic immediately set in. Barry was pounding on the steering wheel and swearing, Vally was screaming at him to turn the car off, and Ben and I were both trying to get the same door open. It was the closest physical contact that we'd ever had; our hands, arms, and legs were all over each other as we tried to get out of the moving car, but it was too late. We were flying over the cliff's edge, wiping out small trees, shrubs, and everything else in our path as the car banged, bumped, and flew toward the skating rink below! Flashes of hockey players in red and black, and purple and yellow jerseys, scattered in every direction when they saw us hurtling toward the rink. The car came to a sudden stop, smashing into, then lodging on top of, a rock. The driver's door creaked open and Barry staggered out; Vally fell out right behind him, wearing only her pink angora sweater; the rest of her was completely naked. I pretended to be unconscious.

Hockey players, coaches, and spectators all gathered around the dinged and scratched car. Ben and Barry were doubled over, laughing like a pair of lucky idiots, knowing it could have turned out a whole lot worse. They seemed oblivious to Vally, who was still lying on the ground where someone had decorously placed his coat across her nakedness. The wailing of an ambulance grew closer, as I hiked my still-virgin ass up the long and dark hill.

Like a brushfire, the story took on a life of its own, and I was branded as a slut—ironic since I remained for the foreseeable future much like the Sahara Desert, large and unexplored.

6

Speeding to the Waistland

Diet #7 ✦ **Benzedrine**

Cost ✦ **A hole in my soul**

Weight lost ✦ **50 pounds**

Weight gained ✦ **0**

We moved again. My mother had found a house she loved but once again couldn't afford. This time, however, she installed my father in the basement under the pretense that he and I needed to know each other better because he was getting old. In truth, she wanted him to pay for half of the mortgage. She also made it clear, in no uncertain terms, that we were moving because it would soon be time for me to go "husband shopping" and that I would want to be in the "right store" and this was a terrific neighborhood filled with the sons of the well-to-do families. She really did think that way.

I was twenty and *still* a virgin, *and* living at home. There should have been velvet ropes around me as I was an "unnatural curiosity"—and I was plenty pissed off about it. This was not how I had seen my life unfolding. I still carried the remnants of my Anastasia phase, believing that I should be attending balls with handsome men throwing themselves at my feet, but there was no one. Was it really because I was fat that I was being locked out of the game? I had an uncanny knack for getting men to befriend me and I was in danger of being crowned, "Queen of the Best Friend Club." But I didn't want to be their best friend. Fuck brains! Fuck personality! I wanted someone to fuck *me!*

Hey, I was young, needy, and not yet the evolved woman it took more than a 101 humiliations to create.

I had to find out, once and for all, if the status quo could be altered if I were to simply disappear and in my place stood a new thin me. Once again, I decided to go on a diet, but this time I was dead serious. My mother gave me an intense top-to-bottom appraisal and shook her head, suggesting I was fine the way I was. She said that I just had big bones, which came from her side of the family; they were all strong like oxen. "Did you just say I looked like an ox?"

My mother became my drug pusher, furnishing me with a never-ever-ending supply of Bennies—Benzedrine, a big-time amphetamine—along with her favorite laxative, Cascara. At last we shared a mother/daughter activity.

I felt as if I were an archeologist; every day I discovered a new bone, and when I caught my reflection in a mirror I had to go back and check if it was really me. I was, however, hopped out of my mind and there was no sitting still to be had. I could not stop moving; I think I even whirred when I walked, and when I talked it was without a filter and at warp speed. I started chain-smoking, too, and I was dropping pounds and barely sleeping . . . but I kept on taking those pills. All good, right? I had to get all new clothes, and when I saw people I knew and said, "Hi" to them, it was more than a little disconcerting to see them look right past me to find out where that familiar voice was coming from.

I got my first bathing suit—up until then I had worn things with skirts and hoods—and I took to the privacy of our garden to tan my blue-white body, which had never before been seen in public. I slathered myself in baby oil and held a giant piece of foil under my chin to reflect as much tanning power as possible up to my face. I was deep into a horse racing dream, in which all the faster horses thundered past me and my swaybacked nag. I leaned forward in an approximation of a real jockey, only I was wider than they were tall, and my cranky horse knew it and he reared up, throwing me to the ground. I was being dragged around the track, gathering mouthfuls of mud and gravel when I was snapped awake by my neighbor's brother, who had been mowing their lawn. "Sorry to wake you, but you were thrashing about and I was worried you were about to fall off that chaise." It took me a moment to come to. I thought I was still sleeping as I stared at the very handsome stranger leaning across the fence.

My brain and body kicked in at the same moment. "Oh my God! I'm wearing a bathing suit and I have drool on my chin." I wasn't sure if I said this out loud or just in my head, but he was laughing. The flush of embarrassment was dueling with the encroaching crispiness of my skin. I tried to cover up by laying the reflector lengthways, which made the sun beat down even harder. Hal introduced himself as my neighbor's youngest but most accomplished brother. More words were spoken; some of them by me but they all hung in the air with no place to land until I heard him invite me on a date.

I was in shock! "Why?" He gave me a strange look but this was all new to me, as I had always done the asking.

Still looking puzzled, he said, "I thought we'd have fun together."

He was a lot older than I was: I was twenty with all the experience of a ten-year-old, and he was a gorgeous, self-assured twenty-seven-year-old man who was studying to be a doctor.

My mother went into overdrive, "A doctor!" She made me a hair appointment, and I bought some very expensive white-on-white patterned silk. (It was expensive, even with the discount I received from the high-end fabric shop where I worked as a kind of training ground for my dress-designing future.) Mummy immediately began making me a beautiful but simple new dress, from a drawing I had done and insisted she not deviate from. I wanted no surprise sequins or any other shiny or dangling embellishments of her choosing.

We took the bus all the way downtown in order to buy me a new pair of shoes to go with the dress. After trying on dozens of pretty ballet flats, we purchased heels. The saleslady insisted they made my legs look thinner. Even though I had never worn such pointy-toed, lady-like shoes I loved them deeply and wore them even with my pajamas in order to appear as if this type of footwear was simply part of my daily routine.

My mother continued to fuss about, picking out just the right old-world jewels from her secret treasure box. A rose gold and pink tourmaline necklace formerly belonging to some rich aunt was the winner. She was like those mice attending to Cinderella, fluttering everywhere, only more like a Prussian diva on crack. She didn't stop her prepping and primping with me, she also sent my father out for a trim, then had her hair lightened and makeup done. She coated her eyes with a heavy silver dust and when she was finished, everything shimmered as though she was on an episode of Star Trek. Even the sofa got new throw cushions. It was as if a head of state was coming over and the only thing missing, thank God, was a red carpet and a marching band. All the bridge ladies were banned for the big night; "Monica has a date. He's going to be a doctor! He's very handsome and he likes her."

It seems that in every neighborhood across the universe, there is always one street where that infamous odd person lives and everyone knows which house to avoid. Sadly, in my neighborhood, it was mine. My father—who was no spring chicken when he had his one and only brief Big Bang moment with my mother, resulting in my birth—was now old and doing "old people" things. He would stand lurking in the shadows behind the curtains, just waiting for little kids to breach the sanctity of our property by letting even a toe touch our grass. If they did, those curtains would fly open, "Private property! No trespassing! Go on . . . go on . . . have a move on!" The curtains would snap back and the terrified children would run home and spread the word. No wonder they all clutched each other's hands and hurried past our house on the way to or from school.

My father stood on sentry duty even though we all knew that my date would soon be coming to pick me up. My mother barked, "Get away from the window. Sit! Sit now! Your daughter has a date and you must not be strange!"

The impossibly good-looking Harold arrived to major fanfare even though I had warned both of my parents to act normal—a description that eluded both of them. My father harumphed and stared him down as if he were a Scotland Yard inspector. My mother coquettishly circled Hal, taking his hand in hers and batting her glittery eyes. Hal smiled back at her. I thought she was going to faint. He was a god, wearing a yellow turtleneck with a wooden Tiki hanging around his neck. I had on my beautiful new white, sleeveless cocktail dress with half my hair piled high in a teased and hair-sprayed bucket, threaded with a white nylon cord that I thought made me look very chic, in spite of the beginning evidence of peeling skin peeking out on my shoulders. After the brief introductions, I hustled him out the door and right into his convertible, and Hal smoothly backed out of our driveway without impaling a single flowerbed. Dick wasn't going to be able to lodge any complaints on this night. The stars were out in full twinkle and my long blonde hair was actually blowing in the right direction—straight back. He had his arm stretched straight out and it was kind of touching my shoulder. I closed my eyes as we sped down the highway, the scent of a warm summer night permeating the air, and I realized I had never had a dream this good.

We went to dinner at the kind of restaurant I had always imagined me walking into: white tablecloths, linen napkins, candlelight and fresh flowers, the room buzzing with a constant hum of sophistication. Hal pulled the chair out for me, then ordered a rum and cola for him and a Singapore Sling for me. He asked if I liked Steak Diane; I had no idea what it was but even if I did, I could barely speak. All my consonants were colliding and I was terrified of making a fool of myself, so I just smiled and hoped that would pass for some kind of answer. Then Hal asked me if I liked Thelonious Monk. Holy crap! Was Thelonious Monk a famous priest, an author? Or could it be a movie? I didn't want to fail this test; I tossed my head back and went for it, "I like him." Hal was pleased, thank God, and he smiled and gently touched my burnt shoulder.

The waiter brought the Steak Diane to the table and poured brandy over it, struck a match, and set it alight. I was mesmerized with the absolute brilliance of my life at long last, when Hal suddenly picked up the water pitcher and *threw* the contents at my head! I was dumbstruck in horror as my beautiful bucket hair collapsed; my false eyelashes came unglued and stuck to my cheeks as my mascara ran down my face, mixing with newly forming tears. I was at dinner with a maniac! The other diners stared in disbelief and alarm. Hal reached across the table with his napkin and I drew back sharply, when I heard him say something about my hair having been on fire. The cord I had used to so fashionably wind through my hair had caught a spark from the flambé and set my hair ablaze. The acrid smell of burned hair and synthetic ribbon wafted around me as I made my escape to the ladies room. I looked at my reflection in the mirror feeling embarrassed and stupid but I did my best to pull myself together, wiping the mascara from my face and tossing the soggy caterpillar-like lashes down the toilet. I still looked like something dragged up in a fisherman's catch, but as I walked from the ladies room toward my table there was a spontaneous round of applause. I was too mortified to acknowledge anyone and wanted to leave the restaurant as soon as possible.

Hal insisted I could clean up at his sister's house nearby as she was in Florida. I waited downstairs while he went upstairs to fetch a towel and when he returned he very sweetly dried my hair, then pulled me toward him and kissed me. I pulled away but then felt stupid for being such a baby, so I kissed him back. But his kisses quickly became more insistent, hard, and brutal, and I felt blood bruising my lips. I was stunned that this was happening. I wrenched free but only for a moment, when he grabbed me and pushed me against the front door, his hands pulling at the zipper of my dress as he pushed into me. I tried to pull away but he had me pinned. "Please don't. Please ... Stop." He lifted my skirt and shoved his hands between my legs, I fought hard but he was so much stronger than I was. "Stop! ... Please ... I want to go home." He ignored my pleas and grabbed my hair, pushing me down onto the floor. He got on top of me, pinning my arms to my sides, ripping my panties as he forced himself into me. I tried to crawl away, but he was not done.

I didn't speak the entire way home. Harold twiddled with the radio to fill the awful silence. At one point he reached across the wide expanse of seat to stroke my hand. I yanked it away and huddled closer to the door. He had barely pulled up to the curb in front of our house, when I leapt from the car and went inside.

I tiptoed into the house where my overly excited mother was dozing in the dark, waiting. She couldn't contain herself, wanting all the details of my fabulous night with the handsome doctor. "It was fine, nice. I'm tired." I wasn't ready to tell her that when I went to Hal's house to dry off, he somehow interpreted that as an invitation to rape me.

I shut the door to my room. I wanted to be dead. It was when I undressed that I saw a spot of blood on my precious new shoes. I threw them into the back of the closet, never to be worn again. I sat on the edge of my bed, unmoving for what seemed like hours. I don't remember having any thoughts. I was numb. When I was sure both my parents were sleeping, I showered in near scalding water until I was so exhausted I was either going to drown or have to get out. I climbed into bed and slept.

I woke up, startled by light flooding into my room as Queen Elizabeth flung open the curtains. I would have preferred she had bricked me in. She stood at the foot of my bed, a shit-eating grin stretched across her face, proffering a bouquet of roses. "He sent you roses; he likes you." I wanted to tell her I hated him but I knew better, she was already planning our wedding.

I stayed in my room for three days, existing on emergency rations: chocolate bars, bread, cheese, and lots of chips—all kinds. None of it made me feel any better but I knew I didn't want to be thin anymore. I needed food, lots and lots of food, and I didn't care if it was good for me, in fact, I wanted it to be poisonous. I didn't want to feel anything.

Hal called every day but I wouldn't talk to him. Each time my mother would shake her head in confusion and disgust. Donna, Beverly, Vally, and all my other friends called wanting details. Did we kiss? Are we going out again? I pretended I had the flu and needed to sleep; I couldn't tell any of them what happened. I threw the Benzedrine away; what did I need diet pills for? But coming off the little black and white pills only added to my misery and I began to shiver with a relentless feeling of coldness that wouldn't go away. I finally crawled out of my cave and made my way to the kitchen, still in my ratty bathrobe, making sure to avoid any room that had windows overlooking Hal's sister's house, in case he might be visiting. I knew I would never set foot in our back garden ever again unless it was under the cover of darkness.

I made cookies and ate the batter, then made more and ate them as soon as I pulled them from the oven, burning myself but barely noticing. I had chocolate chip goo all over me, like some Betty Crocker version of Hester Prynne, only my scarlet letter was brown, my sin worn on my chest for all thin people to see and there was a chorus of them shrieking at me all the time, the loudest of them being my mother. She couldn't understand my behavior. She was so sure I finally had it all, a boyfriend who was successful and liked me. "What is wrong with you?" I couldn't tell her, so I just let her think I was moody and weird. She really believed it was me who put a bomb in the middle of it all. "BOOM! Now she has nothing except a lot of new clothes that don't fit." The Trials at Nuremberg had less judgment.

With the fat or without it, I was not the same person. I knew my family loved me, but I couldn't make a case for myself without telling them the truth and that was never going to happen. I was too ashamed, believing that somehow it was my fault. I shoved everything about that night deep into the vault with the hope that it would stay locked away. But the more I buried the pain and shame, the more I needed to feed.

Weeks passed before I finally emerged from my room, no longer dressed in my self-pity pink flannel, now ready to face the world. I knew it was time for me to move on and move out. I was starting to regret my self-loathing eating binge as the weight I had worked so hard to lose was beginning to circle as it hunted for a perfect place to land.

7

A Bitter Aftertaste

Diet #8 ✦ **Sucking It Up**

Cost ✦ **My compass**

Weight lost ✦ **None**

Weight gained ✦ **Yes**

No one likes change; that was certainly true in my world and being thin-ish was clearly too much change for me. Having experienced the price that came with thin, being fat was far safer and the pitfalls that came with it far more familiar. Both my parents freaked out when I said I was moving, as that was a change they were clearly not ready for. My mother practically barricaded the front door. "Nobody moves! This is your home but suddenly it's not enough for you?" She was on a tirade about my room looking like Nagasaki and that I was just playing at being a grown-up. "Who will do your laundry?"

My father had gone pale at the very idea of my leaving, "You can't, mustn't. . . . No, it would be very, very bad. You can't leave me alone with her, your mother. I won't eat."

She picked up the gauntlet, "If he does eat, I'll poison him! You cannot leave me alone with him, it would be like living with a moldy zucchini."

They were terrified to be alone together and it completely overrode what I needed. My choice was simple. Be the good girl and stay and then who'll be the moldy zucchini? Me. Or be the bad daughter and have a shot at finding myself. My mother chose to help me pack by pulling everything off the hangers and throwing it all to the floor. "Take a look around, this is how it'll be in your fancy grown-up apartment." And my father belligerently practiced being alone as he slunk along the edges of the windows like a garden snake, silent and slithering, ever vigilant, desperate to catch any and all offenders who breached his domain.

But I did it. I left.

I had managed to save a chunk of money, given that my every need was taken care of as long as I was willing to live at home with my parents. Beverly had just taken a cool flat in an old house that I think she wished she could live in by herself but couldn't afford on her teacher's salary, so she was thrilled at my decision to join her and our new friend Katja. For me, it was the best medicine to avoid unraveling the ugly tangle that was occupying my mind.

We all have secrets we carry around; some of them are small, carrying no weight at all. Others are heavy, like tightly tied bags of stones, and those are the ones we don't want anyone to know we have, so we shove them far down, trying to bury them. But like fragments of old wars found in farmers' fields, the shrapnel couldn't be contained. My heavy secret was a doozy, so I ploughed it under layers of comfort food.

I was in need of distraction and I had plenty of it, as we were always on the run leaving a trail of messy that none of us cared about. When we went out it was like being with a pair of beautiful bookends: Beverly was the dark, intriguing one; Katja, the sexy hot one; and I was the loud, funny one. I hated being the loud, funny one, but it did attract mindless attention, and attention was what I was after.

Katja's real name was Kathleen and she had a glass eye from a tobogganing accident when she was five, which made her even more exotic. She was very beautiful but she never had any money. Somehow that never seemed to be a problem; whenever she needed some she'd bat her eye—the good one—and magically some guy would materialize with a full wallet. She seemed to have an inexhaustible supply of rich guys; I would have had to tap dance on someone's head to summon that kind of attention. Katja told me she needed a new eye, something to do with the blink control not working. She had a date with someone pleasant and fairly unassuming and I watched fascinated as she moved into full operational mode, flirting, teasing, her voice becoming all husky. She was good and this poor fool whom she didn't even like handed her a wad of money so "poor Kat" could get a new eye. She rewarded him with barely a peck on his cheek. On her way home from her eye fitting at the ophthalmology clinic, she stumbled across a pair of thigh-high purple suede boots in a fancy shoe shop that she just had to have. Knowing she'd find the replacement money for her eye when it came time to make the payment, but figuring the boots may be long gone, she bought them. I would have done the same thing if I had her legs.

I loved every moment shared with these girls. But at night when the parties ended and we all went to our beds, I was left alone to deal with my thoughts: sharp turbulent swings that ricocheted between fantasies of dismembering Hal's body and dumping each piece in a bottomless pit, and feelings of deep shame that I piled on myself for having led him on. Had I led him on? Was my desperation to lose my virginity so transparent that I asked to be raped? After weeks spent in dead-of-night pathological investigation, going over every possibility from every angle, I became my own hung jury. My conclusion: what's done is done. It was time to put it to rest, if only so I could get some desperately needed peace.

My mother called every hour on the hour to complain about how crazy my father was making her, standing at his post in the window like some old dried up rubber tree, or he'd be at his drafting table making meticulous calculations on his "sure thing" inventions that others had patented fifty years earlier. She didn't get how crazy she was making me, but when she realized she wasn't making a dent in my protective wall, she decided to make her case in person. She stood at the threshold of our front door holding a cardboard box of pastel stuffed animals, which she clutched even tighter once taking in the chaos. After a deep breath she stepped inside with a face that registered something akin to revulsion. She trailed one finger over everything looking for dust and then she sat on the edge of our worn but comfy couch, refusing to take her coat off in case something unspeakable had occurred there. Like a ticking time bomb, she held out the box of bunnies for me to take. It was only a matter of seconds before she pulled a couple of them from the box and dangled them menacingly in front of my face. "You begged me for these."

"I was ten! You are looking for a fight but I won't be goaded."

She couldn't comprehend the change in me that had come with my new address, and none of it made any sense to her—me passing on the potential doctor boyfriend and leaving our very safe and clean house with home cooking included. Mostly she needed to vent, "I'm going to take an axe and kill him." I quietly told her I was sorry she was so miserable but he was her husband, not mine, and she had invited him back into her home because she had to have a better address and needed his bankbook to help pay for it. "That's right and I did it for you and I want you to come home to live, where there are no cockroaches and perverts." I had an involuntary reminder of how wrong she was before I made the mistake of laughing. She stood up, impaled me with a look, and left in a huff without saying a word. None of it fazed me. After all, Queen Elizabeth was just being true to herself.

Beverly had gone off with a new boyfriend to climb Mount Kilimanjaro and Katja was just gone but called one morning to ask me to sell her bed as she had met the love of her life. She had called and asked me to do the same thing last month. I didn't. I was standing in front of the fridge debating between making a healthy but unsatisfying salad or just succumbing to the pull of the mac and cheese I really wanted. Just as I was reaching for the macaroni, one of Kat's throwaways called looking for her. I broke the bad news that she was engaged or something but told him to hang in there, knowing she'd be back on the auction block in a week or two. He laughed and introduced himself as Nick, wanting to know who I was. I was about to say no one but then realized . . . I was just a voice on the phone . . . he couldn't see me. *Ta da*. I emerged from my black hole ready to play. I was funny, sexy, and sassy. He was so captivated that we talked for several hours, and the next night he called back to talk to *me*. Before long, those nights morphed into a few weeks. I couldn't wait to get home from work and become *that* girl, the one he was so desperate to meet, the one I was so desperate he didn't.

I remained convincingly Mata Hari-like until one night he asked me if I had a physical impairment. "Are you part lizard, part woman? Is that why you won't meet me?"

I swallowed my panic and laughed as I tossed my head back and went for it, "I am blonde, green-eyed, and fully equipped." He was on his way.

I knew this day would come as I jumped into the shower, washed my hair and blew it out into all its blonde glory, wondering if I took a full bottle of diet pills, did a colonic, stuck my fingers down my throat and threw up everything I had ever eaten, wrapped myself in saran and steamed for . . . forget it, it was hopeless. I was like a Macy's Thanksgiving Day parade balloon: large and colorful, and in danger of exploding. I was so screwed!

I squeezed my body into a full body condom, yanking that bitch up over my hips until I could no longer bend. I could barely breathe, but I hauled that thing up as if it were a Polish kielbasa sausage casing, and then I stood very carefully hoping nothing would fly out. My boobs were pushed up so high they looked like floatation devices. Maybe he was into that; maybe he was different and maybe he wouldn't care. I slid on a black dress knowing full well black magic was what I really needed. The lumps and bumps were definitely smoother but my organs were crushed. I opened a bottle of wine just as the doorbell rang. I sucked in my tummy, but in a nano second of instinctual self-preservation, I answered the door with just my hair showing. "Hi!" Oh God, oh shit . . . he was gorgeous. I tried to get behind a chair but I felt him staring at me . . . His silence was loaded as he looked at me and shook his head. It was subtle but I caught it. I was hurt and angry. "Yup, that's me—part lizard, part female hippo. . . . Oopsie." I actually felt sorry for Nick. He was busted and he was unsure of what to do next. The silence between us just kept widening until I stepped forward, patted his hand, and held open the door. We both shared a polite smile. The wine didn't even have a chance to breathe and *poof* he was gone.

He wasn't different.

In spite of things not working out between Beverly and her boyfriend, she still arrived home euphoric from climbing the mountain to its summit. Katja wasn't far behind her, cavalierly carving another notch on her belt. "Another one bites the dust." I, however, was devastated but in typical fashion I told no one, swallowing my pain with the same fervor as a drunk on a bender, only my poison of choice required chewing—lots of chewing.

Two weeks later, I was home making popcorn when Nick called. "I miss talking to you."

I let out a long held breath. "I miss you, too." We both missed the banter, the flirtation, and the possibility—but that component was gone. Nick wanted a phone buddy to play with. I wanted the man. Our conversations never got back their groove. He asked why I hadn't been truthful. I laughed and responded, "We would have been done weeks earlier. We never would have met."

He said, "You don't know that."

A touch bitterly, I assured him I did. History was funny that way. Our banter had turned into a battle. He went in hard to the crux of it all, "Omission is the same as lying."

I fought on the side of survival, throwing down the gauntlet, "Say it. Say what you mean. I dare you to name the lie."

The silence got louder. Finally he asked, "Why don't you lose weight; you have such a pretty face."

Blecch! I was in a fury. "I like being fat. I choose it as a fast-track asshole discovery test!" I slammed down the phone. As I stormed out of the kitchen with my incinerated popcorn, I caught my reflection in the toaster and thought, *I am a liar. I don't like my body either.*

8

Bowing to the Master

Diet #9 ✦ **The Master Cleanse**

Cost ✦ **$6.00**

Weight lost ✦ **16½ pounds**

Weight gained ✦ **0 pounds, but crushing insecurity on the rise**

How much more rejection, humiliation, and degradation could I take? I suspected I'd better buckle up, as living with a pair of beauties was not easy on my ego and I often felt like the third wheel, barely hanging on to my seat in a race car being driven full throttle and pretending to love the ride. My job title was clearly "best friend" with nearly identical character traits as described in any dog book under "Labrador retriever."

Labradors have a well-known reputation for appetite. They are persistent and persuasive in requesting food. For this reason, the Labrador owner must carefully control his/ her dog's food intake to avoid obesity. The steady and loyal temperament of Labradors and their ability to learn make them an ideal breed for search and rescue, detection, and therapy work.

Detection, yup, I could always find food and therapy. No, not for me . . . for my friends. Yet, it always surprised me how much they wanted my counsel on so many things and it made me feel appreciated.

Every night I would pray to the Gods of Gravy to leave me alone, and every morning I would begin my day praying for the willpower to not eat. I sat with my hands in prayer pose and summoned Buddha. This was a deity I could relate to, and not just philosophically; *he* was fat! Every morning at the crack of dawn, I would vow to eat clean—a simple piece of toast, a barely there smear of cream cheese, a cup of black coffee, and a medium-size chunk of cantaloupe. But by eleven, the need to feed would be overwhelming and I'd think, *Maybe just a small piece of cheese and a couple of Wheat Thins . . . or four.* When that didn't do the trick, I'd bargain with myself again, *Okay, how about one stick of gum? No, that would just make me salivate, which would make me want more, but more of what?* It didn't really matter because, sooner rather than later, I would cave in to whatever heart-attack snack was on hand, and then would come the cycle of remorse and regret. It wouldn't last, however, because it was in my nature to find the positive in most situations. I was drilling deep to find the upside in being fat. Much like Ivory soap, we fat people float, we retain heat—which makes us great to have around if you become stranded outdoors in wintertime and are in danger of hypothermia—and we are built for comfort, not for speed, which is great when a spare pillow is not available. We are also easy to pick out in a crowd, although not so much in Las Vegas or Germany's fabled Baden-Baden Spa, often filled to the brim with large swim-suited women taking the thermal waters. It's easy to poke fun at anyone who stands out but I knew that for me it wasn't the only way I wanted to stand out. I wanted to be known for my talent, my humor, and hopefully a few good deeds along the road rather than just for my dress size.

There were so many diets to choose from, all making the same promises, but then one day, while standing in the supermarket checkout line, my arms full of potato chips and other snacks, my eye caught a story about several starlets who collectively lost a thousand pounds after a week or so on the Master Cleanse. I was immediately attracted to it as I felt a sense of confidence in a diet with the nerve to label itself as the Master. This was a program that was perfect for me—no food whatsoever. I have always been so much better at dealing with stringent rules without choices; *that* I knew how to do. What I couldn't do was the whole small portion thing. If given any leeway in food choices, this big girl needed big portions. I bowed to my new Master who required loyalty only to the simplest of regimes—ten days of nothing but water mixed with a pinch of cayenne pepper, the juice of a lemon, and a squeeze of maple syrup plus a little dash of herbal laxative mixed in to the drink, followed by a once a day chaser of saltwater. Yum. The first day was easy. I was so into the promise of pounds falling off quickly that I didn't notice any hunger pangs. By the third day my breath smelled like bilge and my eyesight began to falter, but the pounds dropped off like cans of Crisco hitting the deck with a thud, which served to galvanize my will. I was in the zone. I vowed to never eat again. I was one step away from becoming a Breatharian. These people (dare I say, nutcases) believe they can live on air alone without food or water. Unfortunately, there are none around to testify to this—they are all dead.

Temptation was everywhere. I scanned bakery windows fully loaded with sugary, chocolatey temptations all screaming my name. The potent scent of BBQ seemed to be coming through the air vents. Even my beauty products were trying to seduce me: peach facial scrub, Tahitian vanilla-infused body cream, berry scented shave cream, grapefruit shampoo, mint body wash. I wasn't having any of it; I was Mother Teresa and no earthly vanities could toy with my resolve.

I had been invited to yet another engagement party for one of my many girlfriends who had found her mate and was preparing to claim their berth on the ark. I had lost a bunch of weight but I was hardly sylphlike. Still more circular than oblong. *Uggh.* What would I wear? Never easy when a person is fat, dressing well doesn't just happen. There are no easy, "just toss it on and then off we go" moments. Dressing well requires conscious scrutiny and a great deal of careful planning. Tops needed to match bottoms in order to give the illusion of a longer, leaner silhouette. No jumbo florals, or large prints. There was always the danger of being mistaken for an armchair. There's even a temptation to buy clothes several sizes too small, partly because we believe that's how we're supposed to look, and partly because after being on a hundred and ten diets, wish-fulfillment comes into play. We desperately hope that weight loss is right around the corner, so buying it on sale is the smart move—unless the weight doesn't come off or stay off—and even if it eventually does, the jumbo padded shoulders or asymmetrical hemline will be out of fashion. There is nothing worse than a diet begun with the accompanying delusion that makes us run out and buy a whole new wardrobe suitable for a whippet, but we keep every teeny, weeny outfit . . . because we want so badly to believe we will succeed.

Winter is a chubinski's best season; we love quilted down and polar fleece and those shawls and scarves, all of which help to even out the playing field. Everyone looks like the Abominable Snowman. Fall is a great second, we look fabulous in the layered look; after all, we are layered. Spring can be a touch sketchy; the layers are peeled off revealing the truth. The slim girls float around in short pencil-slim skirts and silky nothings, but we are resigned to concealing the damage with artful draping, mostly executed in black, making for large shapeless shrouds accompanied by fabulous jewelry—we know that always fits. The darkest days for fat women occur in the summer because dressing for heat is a nightmare. We shun mini skirts that will reveal our thunder thighs and cellulite; skimpy little tank tops or anything sleeveless will only accentuate the flapping of fat swallowing up our triceps. Shorts are . . . well . . . too short and an invitation to come to the lake or to a pool party just brings on panic; it's the one time burkas make sense to me.

I tentatively dipped into the back of my closet where the thin clothes lived. I pulled them out and apprehensively tried them on. To my absolute astonishment, they were loose!

As exhilarated as I was, I also felt nervous. I had been down this road so often; the compliments, the praise for doing a good job, mostly from mere acquaintances, but the more my body changed, the more uncomfortable everything became as I struggled with the responses of some family and friends who up until now had wanted me to change but, now that I had, didn't seem to like it. There would be gushing compliments that I looked great but I needed to be careful not to go overboard. "You suit a little meat on your bones." "You look fantastic, but don't go crazy buying new clothes. I'd hate to see you throw your money away. We've seen what happened with that plan before." People like us to stay as we have always been no matter what they say to the contrary. It's so much less work for them. My weight loss scared them because I might no longer be the same funny, accommodating, dateless, best friend—me. It scared me, too. It was a case of be careful of what you wish for.

Rewarded as I felt by my success, this transformation was complicated and not always pretty. I had no sense of this me and I didn't know how to handle the sudden onslaught of male appreciation. From the ubiquitous whistles from men holding jackhammers to cabbies, sleazy old guys, and my girlfriends' boyfriends, who now gave me a whole new kind of appreciation. I wasn't used to being objectified. What scared me the most: I liked it. Oh, how I wanted it and oh, how angry it made me that it came because of my new, thinner body.

9

Walking on Water

Diet #10 ✦ **Stress-O-Matic**

Cost ✦ **0**

Weight lost ✦ **0**

Weight gained ✦ **Yes!**

I spent extraordinary amounts of time eyeing myself in any and all reflective surfaces, looking for signs that I was gaining my weight back. I had a history of failures outweighing my successes, so I had good reason to worry. All of it was made worse as I was now designing dresses at my mother's swanky shop—which was filled with mirrors. Being there was akin to making my way through a Gordian knot of demanding clients and gorgeous models, plus having to spend every day with my mother, who was still trying to woo me back to her house. The cherry on the sundae was when she played the "poor Daddy" card: "Your father has gone on a hunger strike and he won't eat till you come home." I didn't want to be unsympathetic, but I refused to be emotionally blackmailed and responded by saying I was on a hunger strike, too, and I needed to live with Beverly and Katja as they were my Holy Grail of inspiration. Living with roommates who were lean, lovely, and very athletically inclined upped my game, meaning I was no longer spending all my time flopped on the sofa.

Beverly and a group of her friends, some of whom were visiting from Germany, asked me to go parasailing with them. I had no idea what parasailing was, but it conjured images of tall-masted sailboats cruising on Lake Ontario on a warm summer day, carrying passengers wearing white pants and navy accessories. I was in; until they explained it was similar to water-skiing, only up in the air. These people were crazy! I must have been drunk or had a gun to my head because I said yes to this adventure, which required wearing a harness *and* a bathing suit! Despite being a thinner version of myself, I still did not have anything close to a body wanting to be on public display in something skimpy. I was now merely plump instead of fat. The word "plump" made me think of smooshy, feather-packed pillows, which did not give me the confidence I needed. Instead, I decided to take on this adventure wearing what I had on: a long pair of pants, a tightly buttoned blouse, and a vest made from some vintage upholstery fabric. But I did kick off my shoes and socks. I'd rather have been hot than exposed. I watched as each of my new friends, one after another, was strapped into a harness; I didn't even like the word "harness" as it summoned images of medieval torture. I was happy to be the gung-ho girl, cheering everyone on as, one after another, they ran along the beach attached to a line being pulled by a speedboat, then skimmed across the water and in a beautiful bikinied ballet they would soar up in the air, arms stretched out with huge smiles of euphoria beaming from their faces. The ride was only a few minutes long but each one of them landed smoothly and gleefully on their feet on the sand, filled with a feeling of conquest. It was now my turn, but I didn't want to go. I was filled with a feeling of foreboding, which one of the Germans said was just a euphemism for fear. *So what if it is, Dr. Freud-Bigmouth?* I thought defensively, but I succumbed to the barrage of assurance from everyone, telling me I would love it, and that it was a piece of cake.

I tried to think of cake as I walked to my execution. I refused to take off the layers of clothing that I said I was wearing to protect me from the sun, but really were there to act as a barrier to protect me from bathing-suit humiliation. A spacey-looking guy in torn shorts, who looked like he'd spent a great deal of time drinking and smoking questionable things came toward me, harness in hand. "This should hold you, I think. *Oookay* . . . in ya go."

My legs turned to stone in instinctual preservation. "That's a very thin rope," I said nervously. An octogenarian slip of a woman with bright red lipstick whipped by me, tightly secure in her harness, and up, up, and away like a beautiful balloon she ascended into the sky. I was egged-on, peer-pressured, and beaten into submission and I was out of rope and out of excuses. Strapped into the harness of doom, I closed my eyes and prayed; the wind, which up until now had been giving everyone a gentle assist was gone and in its place there was a stultifying stillness. "What does it know ... ?" The boat pulled away from the shore but I didn't skim across the water, I clomped, my feet dipping well below the water line, my pants sopping wet up to my knees but the boat still struggled, as did I without any wind to get liftoff. But then in a sudden burst, it took off at warp speed—not in a gentle balletic move but more in a missile-hurtling-into-space kind of move! I *screamed* skyward, my clothes flapping like a flag and my face torqued against the wind in a full-on fright mask, but then, for one nanosecond, I felt the joy. I was flying and I was ecstatic. WOW! But why was the water getting closer? Why did I see open-mouthed horror on Beverly and all the German's faces? People were running toward the water, their hands clasped over their mouths to muffle their panic. *SPLASH!* I was down and under water, I felt the parachute and the heavy harness straps and all my clothes pulling me down, far down. I kicked hard as I pushed and fought my way to the surface, fighting not to drown. I was thinking, this could only have happened to a "big girl" like me.

The rope snapped and I popped to the surface, gasping for air. I heard loud voices coming from the boat as the spacey guy and the boat driver argued; "I thought I told you to get the boat fixed!"

"I thought you were gonna do it!" The boat had stalled, which was not my fault, but with yet one more memorable humiliation, I was hauled back into the boat like a beluga whale and towed to shore.

I took some small pleasure in watching the shocked faces of my friends when I made the decision to go up again with another boat. I had already experienced the worst that could possibly happen and I needed my clothes to dry, but this time when I took off, the wind was at my back and I soared upward, grinning from ear to ear and flying high. When the ride was done, in spite of the little powerboat coming close to shore, a picture-perfect slow arc and the parachute gracefully fluttering down, I somehow managed to land flat on my ass—but it was at least on the sand. I stood up, dusted myself off, and took a bow.

I loved working in Yorkville. It was the dawning of the official love-in for the Age of Aquarius and there were countless tribes of young people flaunting their love beads and free-love lifestyle all over the world but it coalesced in my little part of Toronto's nirvana in a big way. Coffeehouses, paper flowers, and macramé wall hangings, bikers and hippies were all hanging together in formerly staid old Victorian houses that now sprouted hot colors of pinks, yellows, and purples, and out of every one blasted a new and raucous form of music.

Smack in the middle of the mayhem stood my mother's shop, one of many new-style boutiques, dominated by a European coffeehouse at the center of a large courtyard filled with tables of young and happening people—and I had a window on all of it. Mostly I was focused on a shaggy-haired young American draft dodger named Jake who had designs on becoming an actor. He didn't know many people. Born and raised in Brooklyn, he had taken his draft notice with the attached subway token, which was supposed to get him to the nearest army office to declare himself, but instead he had used it to get to the bus station and then into Canada. I had never heard of Vietnam but now I studied up in order to be able to seem informed and caring, my singular and not so politically correct motivation was that Jake was really cute and I wanted to impress him. I joined peace marches outside the U.S Consulate where I met lots of lost boys, most of them lonely and idealistic. They had found their Mother Courage in me and I was only too happy to be their tour guide, even letting a few of them sleep under the wedding dresses in my mother's shop as long as they rolled up their sleeping bags and got out before 9 AM.

Jake and I spent many nights hanging out, debating the war with a motley mix of dissenters and baby right-wingers. Even though we were both on the same side, our arguments were necessary in order to keep the flirtation heady and alive—until one night when it was just Jake and me under the wedding dresses, and there was no more talk of right and wrong. More than being completely spontaneous, it was my first time having consensual sex ever and I was scared. But Jake was no Hal; being with this gentle conscientious objector to all things to do with war, but never to love, gave me back a missing piece of me, along with some subversive pleasure in having done *it* right under my mother's nose.

My life had begun and I couldn't have felt a greater sense of belonging than being smack in the middle of the emerging patchwork of artists, actors, young law students, boutique owners, filmmakers, models, and gadabouts. I had found the circus I was intended to be a part of and I had a ringside seat. I wanted to make sure nothing changed so I was careful and ate cautiously, weighing everything, making sure there was no fat, no salt and most often, no taste. I didn't care; I needed to remain vigilant in order to remain thinner, which allowed me to remain happy—but also perpetually hungry.

I was half asleep thinking those dreamy, forbidden early-morning moist-making thoughts: *Mmmn . . . Oh yeah, crispy bacon, cheesy eggs, thick buttery toast . . .* when the phone shrieked next to my ear. I didn't need to be psychic to know it was my mother; it was always my mother and she always woke me up. I had visions of her pacing like a caged animal until she thought it was a reasonable time to call. It was never reasonable; if roosters weren't up then neither should I be, but she was sounding more agitated than usual. "I need you to talk to your father, he listens to you." I explained that was because I listened to *him* but she was already off and running, "Three times, he calls my name. He's stuck in the bath, his arteries are filled with seventy-five years of rice pudding . . . he knows he cannot have baths. He knows this, he gets stuck, he's like a mountain of wet papier-mâché and I have to go in there, bend down, and touch that . . . piece of white putty. He's like an albino. English men must never take off their clothes. I had to wrap my arms around him and lift him from the bathtub. These are supposed to be my golden years?"

I muttered under my breath, "And his rust ones." I promised I'd be there in an hour.

The paramedics were just packing up; it had been a mild stroke but I knew it was just the beginning. With me gone, so was the glue. My father needed care and my mother was my mother. They were like two people with rubber cement under each of their shoes; no matter how hard they wanted to escape from the prison of their own design, they couldn't.

Whoosh! And in the speed of light, I was back home living in a bedroom that no longer belonged to me, filled with memories that

I didn't ever want. It struck me as perfectly paradoxical given that my mother had almost sent out a daughter-wrangler to get me back home, that exactly at the same time, she had managed to turn my not-so-old room into a repository for all of their out-of-season clothes, old tax papers, and books. There was a terrifying box filled with pointy frozen-faced, glass-eyed foxes sewn together with heads and tails all out of order that she wore when grand occasions arose that required evening stoles and muffs. Muffs? I had awful dreams filled with animals, their faces still attached, casually tossed over my mother's shoulders. I woke up sweating and threw the box of foxes into the basement. Where would she have worn those—to some Bavarian opera in hell?

It was true; one can never go home again. Nearly instantly I felt the stress bubbles percolating. It started almost imperceptibly with a need for a small bite of cheese, just a nibble. That nibble sprang into a full-blown craving, that craving then became manic as I shoveled almost half a round of Havarti into my newly pristine gullet. I didn't even enjoy the taste as it went in and down so quickly. I followed that with a quick trip to the nearest grocery store where, as I gathered my emergency supplies, I consumed half a fresh baguette, some olives, a few grapes, maybe . . . just a little chocolate, and this was all before getting into the checkout line where telltale crumbs stuck to me as witnesses to my crash.

I was twenty-three years old, living with my mother and father who were allergic to each other and went out of their way to bully and bribe me into being on their side and *boom*, I fell right back into my old routine, eating fatty foods from a long-gone empire and loving the familiarity of every bite. My mother's cooking always began with the sizzling sound and smell of chicken fat, pork fat, butter or Crisco, and this was before the cream cheese or bread-crumbing began. In some homes the daily ritual consisted of saying a prayer before every meal; in my home the ritual was to have a cream-filled dessert after every meal. Fruit was canned, vegetables were frozen, and all meat was baked until grey. I succumbed so quickly to giving up my newly carved out independence and reverted to being right back in the middle of the well-traveled footbridge between my mother and my father's wants and needs. The latest foray was my mother's request—meaning demand—that my father sort through his things in case something were to happen to him so that she would know what things really mattered. What did she mean by "if something were to happen" to him?

My mind flipped to black and white, as in a 1940's film noir: My father, skeletal from not eating, sits in a wheelchair behind the lace curtains waiting for someone to make his day. My mother arrives home. She has a hammer in one hand and carpet tacks in the other as she opens the door and silently walks to the curtain, then hits him sharply on the head. He slumps over and she drags his withered carcass out of his wheelchair and onto the floor where she nails his body in the exact position he has fallen. She begins to walk over him, over and over until he's flat as a bearskin rug. She's smiling as she reaches for the vacuum cleaner.

The gnawing, searing, need to feed was back! I knew it would happen; it always happened as soon as I hit even the smallest of bumps in the road. In order to live a fat-free life, I would have to live in a Zen garden in Bhutan where possibly a life could be lead with no stress. But I'd always be struggling in this one. "*Ommmmmmm, Aaaarrrrrgggghhhhhhhhhhhhhhh . . .*"

I knew how to lose weight! I had done it over and over again. I had a gold star for losing weight and a platinum one for gaining it back: fifteen pounds lost, thirty-five found; sixty pounds lost, a hundred pounds found. Off it came and on it went like a cheesy "lights on, lights off" Clapper, just as it does with 90-plus percent of those who lose weight. But do you ever wonder where the fat goes? Those hundreds of thousands of pounds lost every year—lost and then found. I'm no scientist but I do have a hypothesis. Fat doesn't just disappear. These "fatoms" circle high above the hole in the ozone, just waiting for one bad hair day, one teeny emotional meltdown, a mini-rejection and *WHAM!* Fat always finds its way back home.

10

Shaky ground

Diet #11 ✦ **Bananas and Milk**

Cost ✦ **$14.00**

Weight lost ✦ **4 pounds**

Weight gained ✦ **18 pounds**

I stealthily slipped back into my far more satisfying life with Beverly and Katja, careful to leave a few things lying around my old room in the hope that my parents would think I was simply staying away for just a few days, my closet still filled with enough clothes to fool the eye as I shuttled back and forth between my real life and my obligatory shift work managing my parents, hopefully making enough appearances to keep the ruse going. I was relieved to be back with my friends and on the wagon in an attempt to recover from living in the "food time warp" that I got sucked into at my parent's house.

The bananas and milk diet, which had been around for decades on the top ten celebrity diets list, had made a return appearance, and became the newest crazy fad I embraced. I had always detested milk, but now I had to swallow gobs of the slimy stuff. I tried, really I did, but I couldn't do it, so I made an executive decision and substituted chocolate milk. This was somewhat more palatable, but after four days of nothing but half a dozen bananas and three or four giant cups of chocolate milk, I was not just bored, hungry, and seriously irritable but, worst of all, I was blocked—as in severely constipated. Much of my time was spent rocking back and forth on my bed clutching my stomach as it throbbed and died, like a car that had been fed the wrong kind of gasoline, the rest of the time, I was pacing back and forth in front of the refrigerator and pantry, visualizing every food I craved—and none of them were bananas. I wanted bread, salami, cheese and cake, and I didn't care in what order. On day five, I couldn't look at another banana as they were now the enemy and I treated those little Chiquita's like the betrayers they had become by tossing a whole bunch of them into the backyard composter, giving them the punishment they deserved. Bye-bye bananas! The sickly sweet and slimy chocolate milk was given an equally harsh punishment as it swirled to its death down the kitchen sink drain.

But that wasn't the only kind of blockage I was suffering from. I had shoved the horrible date rape deep under a carpet of food and denial, taking on all the shame and even some of the blame. I knew intellectually that it wasn't my fault but that didn't stop me from a daily dose of emotional self-flagellation. I knew I should talk to someone, but the dishonor I felt was too big to share so I buried it deep down in the vault for another day.

If one's body was one's temple, I'm pretty sure mine would have to have been considered a teardown; I was my own slumlord. I was in need of chocolate and lots of it, as in deep, dark, soothing, mind-numbing chocolate. I had a spiritual ritual when it came to eating chocolate and no Hershey's crap need ever apply. My chocolate had to be a silky, crave-worthy temptation, a dangerous and potent siren that called out to me, and I had a seductive ritual to consume it. I would slowly take off the outer wrapping and place the foil-wrapped bar between my thighs just long enough to get it to just the right texture, still hard but creamy-dreamy, mouth-meltingly perfect. Potatoes were my other solace-inducing, go-to antidepressants. I didn't care if they were baked, roasted, mashed, scalloped or the most tantalizing of all, heavily salted and french-fried. *"Aaahh"* I would become weak at the knees at the oh-so familiar taste that would soothe me into a sense of tranquility.

Normally, I wasn't dumb enough to go out with my two hot and sexy best friends, but the deadening effects of a full stomach sometimes clouded my judgment. So once again we went to a club and the mating ritual began within minutes, with Katja swept off her feet by some poseur playboy and Beverly face-to-face in chemistry with her beautiful male doppelganger, leaving me to dance with all the pretty gay boys who loved me just the way I was. I was having a perfectly wonderful time despite knowing that when the clock struck midnight, whomever was making me feel so special would be out the door with someone slim and trim with a mustache. I was on the dance floor, pulsing to the music when a slow tune came on and everyone began to pair off. I was conspicuously alone, no longer able to pretend to be part of the crowd.

I made my way over to the jammed-up bar and within minutes I accidentally made eye contact with one of the most beautiful men I had ever seen. He had the kind of naturally streaked blond hair that women pay big bucks for, a heartbreakingly warm smile, and vivid blue—nearly turquoise—eyes. He took my breath away, along with every other man-hungry guy's and girl's alongside me. I knew I would have to bump off every one of them to stand a chance of getting marginally close to this man even for a second. *Why does one never have hemlock or eye of newt when one needs it?* I prayed I wouldn't have to resort to hostage-taking, but then he motioned for me to dance with him. *Sigh* . . . of course, he must be gay.

The music was pulsating, the lights were strobing, and I was gyrating with blissful abandon as he and I danced three more dances. I had no breath left and thought I was going to die of a heart attack but I wouldn't be the first to quit. I felt faint and thirsty. Thank God, he threw his hands up in defeat and returned to the bar. I tossed my hair around and kept up the pretense of dancing, but then he waved me over. I checked to make sure he meant me. He thought that was funny and handed me a drink—we still hadn't said a word to each other but he had a beautiful smile and a very direct gaze that made me feel weak in the knees. It didn't take long for me to discover he didn't speak a word of English. I made a vow to only pick up young men fresh off the boat from there on in. He was "Johann from Amsterdam" and on the flip side, I still didn't really know if he was gay or straight.

I offered to show him the town, which culminated in a visit to my place so I could show him off to the girls. Up until then, I had always been the date-o-meter for Katja's pickings. Whenever she'd bring a new guy back to our place, she would ask me to join them for a short while so I could assess his worthiness. Inevitably and quickly I'd give him a thumb's down, as they were mostly creeps and cretins. Kat had terrible taste in men. Beverly usually was savvy and careful with her choices so I hadn't had any to worry about with her. But the minute Johann stepped across the threshold of our house, it was obvious that neither Kat nor Beverly approved. I chose to block my ears and tune out their misgivings. I did the justification quickstep, so sure they didn't know him the way I did.

I introduced Johann to all my favorite cafes, bars, and shop owners. He knew how to charm everyone, and I was in heaven as I followed in the wake of this spectacularly good-looking specimen. In some unrealistic way, I believed his aura washed over onto me, casting me in a prettier and better light, one that made him choose to hang out with me. But still, I was gob-smacked that he wanted to spend more and more time with me and I allowed myself to fall deeply in love. Soon, he began spending nights at my place. At last, I had a man in my bed and all of Katja and Beverly's suspicions were ignored. I actually believed they were jealous. What I didn't know was that he was thrilled to be out of the crowded hostel he'd been living in and my place was perfect for his needs. I think even if I had known, I would still have allowed myself to ride the wave—in case it was one that was never going to come to my shores again.

It didn't take long for the gloss to fade. If my self-esteem was fragile before, it was now Code Red as I came to understand that I was in love with a man who preferred sleeping with a mirror more than with a warm body. Johann was a model. Shoot me now! How perfect for him that I was a dress designer and *knew people*. I was so happy to introduce him to everyone I knew that could help him and it wasn't long before he began to get one fashion gig after another. On the downside, I was anointed with the less than glamorous position of sherpa: his personal 24/7 *schlepper*. I had a car and I came to understand how valuable this commodity could be, as I drove Johann to his go-sees—auditions for modeling jobs. I delivered, picked up, and often paid for his dry-cleaning, and ferried his massive wardrobe back and forth to wherever he was shooting.

To hang with him, I had to hang with his new friends who were all picks of the litter, meaning other *fahboolus* models. I dragged giant wardrobe bags, enormous tool-chest-like containers filled with hairspray, special brushes, tweezers, nostril-hair clippers, and gallons of water to dazzling locations where I thumbed distractedly through countless magazines, which featured the very people I was waiting on, while Johann, Yanka, Vibecka, Tiiu, and other exotic giraffe-like creatures were primped and polished before being posed in unnatural positions on freezing cold beaches in winter—but propped to look like summer—and to ski slopes in summer made of mashed potato flakes piled mountain high. I liked those shoots, knowing that if I were desperate, I could just add hot water and salt and I would be able to feast for weeks. Johann was not the brightest penny in the purse but he was smart enough to thank me over and over for all that I did for him, which was pretty much everything except cut his meat into bite-size pieces.

What the hell was wrong with me? He was a divine genetic creation put on this earth to make mere male mortals feel inferior, and I already believed I was an inferior, clearly made not in God's image but more likely in his Latvian housekeeper's. Johann was so full of himself it didn't matter; he never noticed. He didn't see me. I even went back on the dreaded bananas and milk diet in the hope that if there was less of me, he might come to love me. Ha . . . not ever. He was already in a committed relationship with himself.

I may have been insecure, but I wasn't stupid, and when I caught him cheating on me with a woman old enough to be his mother, I packed all his clothes and put them outside the front door. He assumed that she could help him even more than I could because she owned a big-time modeling agency. Johann from Amsterdam didn't understand, but this time it wasn't a language problem. He just couldn't believe I was throwing him out. I could. I was deeply grateful to both Beverly and Katja for not rubbing my nose in one of the endless plates of leopard-spotted bananas that began piling up in our trash bin.

Brokenhearted as I was, I was also filled with a sense of relief at having escaped from the very tall, very thin, shiny-haired nomads who wandered the earth with one hand always on their hips and hand mirrors ever present in the other, followed always by legions of fluffers and an ever present camera crew. I decided to concentrate on my career as a dress designer. If I was going to be alone, I'd better be able to afford me, seeing as I liked nice things. I painted the interior of my mother's shop pink and purple, telling her it would be good for business. It was. My mother's store had become a happenin' boutique in the middle of Toronto's version of Haight Ashbury and I was turning suburbanite *hausfraus* into fake flower children. I had these old women of forty wearing granny dresses, fringed vests, and John Lennon little round glasses. I was a star in the world of weekend hippies, if having a following of gay boys and old broads from the boonies was your thing. Given that I was once again in recovery from another unhealthy attraction, having any kind of following was a relief.

Beverly had originally rented our small flat for herself but then Katja moved in and my arrival only added to the chaos. It was fun at first, but with three girls and all their clothes and makeup plus whatever guys the other two were madly in love with, and then me with the model boyfriend and all his paraphernalia, it had become similar to living in a clown car. We loved each other but we were all vying for space in front of the same mirror, shower, and ironing board—and that had only one potential outcome. None of us wanted to live through a Bay of Pigs incident of our own making, so we decided to go house hunting.

We had very limited funds as Beverly was a schoolteacher, I was a junior dress designer who was underpaid—under the table by my mother—and Katja never had a real job, bouncing from one reinvention to another as they often interfered with her far more interesting love life. Her latest "career" was as a photographer scouting for a local newspaper's Sunday hunk-of-the-week picture. It was a bad move for Katja, who was catnip to men of all ages and capable of loving each and every one.

Beverly and I found a sweet, albeit even more run-down, but much bigger house in a great neighborhood, and on the day we signed the lease Katja was fired. Each week she'd fallen in love with whichever hunk she was photographing, making her perpetually exhausted and continuously late, which meant Beverly and I were on the hook for all of the rent if Katja didn't find another job soon. She did, but it was as a tour guide to all those who wished to visit the unexplored Third World. Before she left, she told me she had met a guy who she thought would be perfect for me. My heart thumped a bit faster, no one had ever offered to fix me up before. I excitedly asked her what he looked like, what had she told him about me, and why was he perfect for me? She looked confused, then realized that she had made me think she was fixing me up on a blind date. Instead she wanted me to meet a guy who had just started a television station and was looking for unusual ideas. Now I was confused. Katja explained that she thought it would be amazing if I did an exercise show. She told the guy I was big, but the most limber person she'd ever known. She gave me a hug and then said his name was Moses. "He'll call you," and with that she was gone. I wasn't sure whether to be insulted or flattered, and I already had a career. It was time to find a new roommate. Bye-bye Katja.

And so batty Patty entered our lives bringing chaos and crazy with her. I met Patty at a party and she seemed warm and engaging, if a bit wild. During a break in a beer-quaffing contest with some other revelers, I overheard Patty mention she was desperately looking for a place to live. No due diligence was done, other than asking her if she had a paying job, which she did. She told us she did very well selling gardening supplies and had done it for years. We were ecstatic to have solved our problem and invited Patty to move in. She neglected to tell us she would be accompanied by a pair of destructive cats who loved nothing more than shredding anything soft, meaning our curtains, our sofa, and a few of our coats. It didn't take long for our new home to look like we lived in a string factory. Beverly and I wanted to cook the damn cats in a stew along with the shredded sofa bits, but Patty's monthly cash contribution was more important to us than the horror of newly fringed furniture, so we said nothing. Then, out of nowhere Patty accused me of wearing her clothes, which could only have worked if I was wearing her sweaters as ankle warmers. Patty was 5'9" and slender as a willow tree, whereas I was 5'6" and as round as a stump. She habitually flung crazy and paranoid accusations in all directions and Beverly and I tried to stay out of their trajectory, but when her dealer showed up at our back door at 2 AM demanding payment for a shipment of weed, we understood why she was bonkers and what kind of garden supplies she was *really* selling. Bye-bye Patty.

There wasn't even time to spread the word that we had a vacancy before Beverly announced she was leaving her job, her life, and me, to go live with Gunnar, a boy she had met while climbing Mt. Kilimanjaro with her previous boyfriend. I was happy for her but devastated; she was my best and most trusted friend. Bye-bye Beverly.

I was feeling scared and abandoned. I couldn't afford the house on my own but none of my close friends needed a place to live. I wasn't ready to try anyone new but I also didn't want to have to move back into my parent's nightmare. So, I found a second job selling fabric in a very exclusive shop in the same area as my mother's boutique, and I shuttled back and forth between the two. At night when I'd get home I was exhausted, and the idea of folding anything after hours of rolling, straightening, and tidying both stores was anathema to me; I didn't care if my clothes piled up into mountains or if my home looked like it was inhabited by rabid pack rats. Somehow I knew my mother was gloating at her prophecy now fulfilled. I ate anything and everything as long as it didn't require cooking. Junk food was the fastest fix, along with spooning straight out of any one of the containers of ice cream I kept stashed in the freezer. Then I'd fall onto the clothes-strewn sofa and pass out from exhaustion.

After a few marathon weeks of long hours, I was almost comatose when my phone rang—some guy called Moses. The name rang a bell but that was all, until he mentioned that Katja had given him my number. He suggested I come down to the television station and we meet, as he was intrigued by my idea. I didn't have an idea, Katja did, and I wasn't sure what it was exactly but I didn't say that and I agreed to meet him.

City Television was not just new, it was an outrageous affront to conventional TV. It was a place where the inmates were running the asylum. It was the brainchild of this man Moses Znaimer and he was unlike anyone I had ever met: brash, bold, and brilliant. I was terrified of him. But being young and completely without any knowledge of how television worked or who should be on it gave me my edge. I spun bullshit into whole cloth as I painted an indelible picture of a fat girl with long blonde hair who could do backbends and the splits while making small talk and, to sweeten the mix, I promised interviews with anyone who thought they were experts in the world of diets and food. I had barely finished what was my first ever "pitch" when Moses dismissed me by saying: "Great can't wait to see your show." *Me too,* I thought . . . *What?* This was crazy but exciting.

It would take a few months to pull this unexpected turn of events together. There was no real money, just plenty of anticipation while I and a group of funny, creative minds brainstormed what was to become a huge change in direction for me. In the meantime, rent had to be paid and dresses needed to be designed, and I needed to stop eating.

11

Starve~a~Palooza

Diets #12, 13, 14, and 15 ✦ **Scarsdale, Clay,
Protein Powder, and Dexedrine**

Cost ✦ **$240.00**

Weight lost ✦ **All of it**

Weight gained ✦ **All of it**

Pressure ... Pressure ... Pressure ... Never had there been so many people pulling me in different directions. My mother was not entirely happy that I was going to be on TV because she was afraid I wouldn't be available to work for her, but then again, she was really happy that I was going to be on TV as it reflected well on her status. When I was driving her on her errands, I was no longer allowed to wait in the car while she carried on her schmooze-fest with her friends in the deli/bakery/butcher, as I was now worthy of being shown off. "Did I tell you Monica is the star of her own television show?" Her friends would all nod and then ask questions about what celebrities I knew and I would try to break it to them that I was not starring in anything yet and I didn't know any. That's when they would turn their backs and go about their business. I could feel my mother glaring at me for not embellishing in the way she had clearly done.

The TV station needed me to be available whenever the studio was free and I shuttled back and forth between there and my two other jobs, one of which I was in danger of losing, seeing as I took so much time off. I pleaded and promised the snotty manager of the fabric store that I would do better and I did. I was firing on all pistons at all of my jobs but once I walked through the door of my house where no one could see me, I crashed and burned. If it wasn't moldy or hard as rock I ate it, along with whatever else I could forage from my poorly stocked kitchen. Candy bars were easy and they became breakfast, sometimes dinner, along with globs of gluey Chinese food from the really horrible neighborhood takeout.

I was passed out, on, or under the growing mountain of clothes and laundry when I heard the jiggling of a key in the door. I woke up and grabbed a snow boot as a weapon as Katja bounced into the room. She had met a pilot in Belize and they were madly in love. Of course they were. She had quit her job and flown back in the cockpit's jump seat and thought she'd surprise me and see if there was room for her to crash for a week or two while the pilot sorted things out with his wife.

Having Kat back was a miracle. She had time on her hands while waiting for her pilot and she wanted to use it to take care of me—because as usual she didn't have any money and this was her way of paying her freight. Clothes were picked up and hung up, and the fridge was de-junked and restocked with healthier alternatives. There was a reason she had an amazing body; she didn't fill it with crap. But I also understood her addictions were just different than mine and we both had plenty of them. She used the time back in Toronto to figure out how to get her new glass eye, which was ready and waiting for pick up as soon as she could pay for it. Much like Scarlett O'Hara, tomorrow was another day and she was sure she would find the money somewhere or from somebody. She had no regrets about blowing the first handout on her fabulous purple boots, seeing as she kicked butt in them all the time. She didn't want to hit up the pilot, even though he had offered, because she had forgotten to collect then and there and she didn't want to jeopardize any sensitive negotiations he might be involved in by calling him at home and having his wife answer.

Kat decided we should throw a dinner party to celebrate the amazing news of my up-and-coming exercise show and her good fortune for having met the true love of her life. I winced. She invited a couple of her old flames with bucks to spare, figuring she'd get the moola that way. Neither of us needed much excuse to throw a party.

From beginning to end, it was a debacle. Katja came home after having been to the optometrist, having convinced them to give her the new eye by promising that she'd bring the money in the next day. I was curious, asking if I could see her new eye before she put it in.

That was the first and last time I have ever said that sentence. She took it out of its box and I was surprised to see that its shape was almost triangular, making sense, as it had to fit into the socket. As weird as it was to be ogling the ogler, I felt honored that she trusted me, but just as I handed it back to her, it slipped to the floor and disappeared in a crevice of the old house never to be seen again, no matter how much we searched, even lifting up floorboards. Kat was far cooler about it than I was. She actually laughed at the idea that at some point after we had moved on, someone would stumble upon it and from then on an outlandish tale would be spun to explain the bizarre find. With a totally blasé attitude, she did a quick calculation, doubling the money she would need as she now would have to pay for yet another new eye as well as the one that had disappeared.

Somehow we thought there were going to be about ten people for the dinner, but in our exuberance, we didn't check with each other about who had invited whom and there were at least forty, making it officially a cocktail party. Neither of us knew how it happened, but we knew we didn't have enough food for a sit-down dinner, so we improvised and made finger food. Everyone brought wine, so most people were too drunk to notice. I didn't really drink, so I noticed, because I was starving—not in a third-world famine kind of a way, but in a deprived food-loving, fat-girl kind of a way, which just left me feeling vulnerable. And after an unexpected glimpse of my body as I walked past the now cleaned and shiny toaster oven, I caught my reflection: It was if a Botero painting had come to life, complete with its exaggerated and disproportionate bulk.

I was shattered and filled with self-loathing and I couldn't shine it on for another second so I went outside and took refuge on a rusty, wrought iron chair in the shadows. The music and raucous sounds of a party coming from inside my house did nothing to soothe my agitation. I sat under the cloudy night sky thinking about how out of control I had allowed myself to become. One look from a passing stranger would have confirmed that I was not currently a happy person.

I must have fallen asleep because when I woke up, with every part of me in pain from having sat for so long, there was a blanket draped across my legs. I untangled myself and stood up, and immediately caught sight of a man with a huge Afro staring at me from his apartment window across the street. I moved to the shadow of the wall and crept inside. Katja was asleep on the couch, amid a sea of debris from the remains of what appeared to be a very successful party. I woke her up and told her to look outside to see if the man was still watching our house. He was. We turned off all the lights and sat in the dark taking turns to see if he had left, meaning he could be headed over to our house, but he was still there, motionless, and watching our every move. We armed ourselves with kitchen knives and took turns being on watch but neither of us could sleep; we were too scared. We called the police but they said a person had every right to be standing at their window. If anyone should have known that, it would be me. When the sun came up, everything looked far less ominous—especially the big-haired man in the window. "He" wasn't a man at all; it was a big, round stationary window fan that wasn't going anywhere. We were slap-happy from relief and lack of sleep, and only a little mortified.

Heading into the kitchen I saw the toaster, which instantly reminded me I needed to make a radical change before I went on television in a leotard. It was one thing to know the camera added ten pounds, but on me that was two five-pound bags of potatoes. So began another foray into full-bore Starve-a-Palooza. I had to find a diet that would allow me to eat on the fly; I was too busy to cook and I also didn't want anyone to know I was on yet *another* diet. Up first was the Scarsdale Diet. It offered up a dizzying spread of the most boring unadorned food anywhere, chicken without the skin, and salads with no dressing. It was a diet plainer than a Quaker's bedroom. But the salads and vegetables were open season with no portion control. Perfect, I had no control and I got my wish—no one would have ever guessed I was on any kind of diet. I ate like a mulching machine until I threw up, and strangely I did start to lose a little weight, likely from feeling continuously queasy from all the artificial sweeteners, which were encouraged in everything from pudding to diet sodas. Dr. Tarnower and I soon parted company; he had not been a cheap date and I wasn't that much thinner. Moving on . . .

I was elated when I discovered the Clay Diet, which sounded blissfully easy with no calories to count and nothing to weigh. It consisted of a cocktail made of a special clay, taken two hours before meals, supposedly giving one that full and satisfied feeling. When liquid Bentonite is taken internally, it rapidly absorbs all fluids in the stomach, causing a feeling of fullness, thereby reducing appetite and any desire to over eat. Yes! Easy peasy. But it wasn't long before I began to feel like I might explode from all that clay. It tasted like a thick stucco-and-water milk shake, not that I had any real frame of reference for what *that* tasted like, but there's a certain kind of smell when you walk into a damp basement and the walls are wet. It's so potent, you can sense the taste and it isn't good. I was sure I was making fat little statues that were now living in my bloated gut.

The show must go on and I was about to make my exercise debut even though the swelling kept getting worse and worse, and there I was, encased in a leotard sitting in a makeup chair next to a very sweet and brilliantly quippy Dan Aykroyd, who was going to be my announcer. It was his first television job, too. I should have been over the moon with excitement but I was feeling like a cement-mixing truck.

It was my first day on a set and it was the camera crew's first time on a set, maybe their first time holding a camera. We were all really young and really clueless but we had enthusiasm and a kind of Gonzo determination to do well. I may have been fat but I was also blessed with an elastic body, and from a very early age, I had brought tears of laughter and amazement to my family with acrobatic antics and contortionist displays. Given that I knew no shame, and seeing as I was willing to try anything, I was sure I would be a success. But on that first day, I was about as flexible as a brick. I covered by talking fast and talking some more, then while attempting a somersault, I picked up a set phone and ordered a pizza and had it delivered while doing the show. It was an amazing day as I again stumbled through an unexpected door and found an unexpected part of me. I was funny.

The show attracted a following that crossed several demographics, a few of them weird. Of course it did, I was a fat girl in a leotard who could stand on her head and still talk. Gilda Radner was a close friend and a favorite guest because she was so damn funny and because she actually thought she was overweight, but as it turned out she was bulimic, a far less common disease then than it is today. I decorated the show's holiday Christmas tree with chicken legs and donuts and I gave a platform to endless experts from nutritionists to psychiatrists. My favorite guest was a psychiatrist who had written a paper claiming that fat people should be gathered together in colonies; that if one could harness the fat stored in all those corpulent bodies, one could heat and light a city the size of New York. I asked him if he had ever touched a fat person and then I took his hand and placed it on my knee. Only putting his hand on a hot stove could have appeared more painful. He stuttered and stammered that he wasn't speaking about me or other "well-adjusted fat people." Once he realized he had a rope around his neck, he shut up. I leaned in very close and said, "Fat people are such easy targets." And then I offered to be on standby as an auxiliary generator if the power supply at my local hospital ever experienced a blackout, if he could just explain how he thought we could actually make his *great idea* a reality. He had no answer. But the best perk of all that I got from doing my show, was that for the first time ever, I won approval for being fat me from my whole family. *Aaah*, fame . . .

Being on the show had another unexpected effect—spending so much time talking about diets and exercise, I began to fear food. It had become the monster I needed to stay far away from, so I was thrilled when I found my next diet, which had no food.

It was the heavily promoted Liquid Protein Diet, which required me to only drink. I found a dealer living in a seedy neighborhood where I handed a woman, who behaved very much like a pre-Cold

War Russian spy, a check for $65.00. The exchange was made and I left with two jumbo plastic bottles filled with the magic potion. Just as I was settling in for my first yummy taste, I happened to pick up the newspaper. The story that jumped out at me was about the ten most recent deaths attributed to the Liquid Protein Diet: not enough amino acids and apparently a few other missing life-giving nutrients. I immediately tossed both bottles.

Then I saw an ad for Dexedrine, a new and vastly improved way to quick and effortless weight loss. Like a junkie with a convenient memory, I completely erased my first unhealthy wild rise on that very same drug, only remembering that it worked and true to its word, it was speedy. Sold! One little pill a day and I had twice as much energy and next to no appetite. Brilliant—but within a week I couldn't stop twitching. I had so much energy that instead of sleeping, I went on cleaning binges—which was good—but that's because I was terrified to go to bed. My nights were filled with apocalyptic nightmares and a constant feeling of foreboding. When my doctor brother-in-law heard what I was on, he didn't mince his words: "Throw those pills away now! They are dangerous, hallucinogenic, and are playing havoc with your heart and nervous system."

For the first time I realized all my diets were beginning to collide, much like a chain-reaction pile-up on a foggy freeway, and I knew I was headed for a serious crash. I had become a diet junkie and at the time there was no rehab for that. If I stayed this course, it was the fast track to becoming a full-fledged, fat anorexic.

12

Out of Control

Diet #16 ✦ **The Last Chance Diet**

Cost ✦ **$130.00**

Weight lost ✦ **34 pounds**

Weight gained ✦ **1 pound but climbing**

My friends were dropping like flies and my social life was taking the hit. They were all getting engagement rings and flashing them in each other's faces, as if trying to blind them with the size, shape, and cut of their diamonds. As their best single friend, clearly I had a neon sign on my head that said, "Always open." One after another they'd come and tell me the most intimate details of their lives: "Should I marry him? He slept with my boss?" "Is he the one, what if I meet someone better?" "What if he finds out I slept around?" How the hell did I become Mother Superior? I was dispensing life advice as if I knew what I was talking about, but I did learn one very valuable piece of information; everyone is screwed up, even the pretty ones, which made me feel a little better.

What wasn't making me feel so great was that I had become everyone's favorite dog sitter whenever they would go off for a romantic long weekend. I love dogs but only the big ones—give me a husky, or a Burmese mountain dog and a flexi-leash, and send me on my way—but most of these doggies were teeny, shrill, yapping machines and they had more clothes than I did. My friend Marlie once asked me to look after Pepsi, her mini Yorkshire terrier. Could there be a dog smaller than a regulation Yorkie? Pepsi lived in a bag, a very fancy leather bag, and he went everywhere with Marlie: to the theatre, to every clothing store, and to restaurants where Pepsi was checked at the cloakroom if the management disapproved of him being under a table. (Who wears cloaks anyway?) Marlie, who was more than a little neurotic, wanted to make sure I knew how to follow Pepsi's routine and therefore wasted a considerable amount of my precious time schooling me in the art of feeding and caring for a dog the size of a teacup. I was a good student and promised to follow all the rules. In our last stop, at the park, Marlie wanted me to see how Pepsi *did her business*. By that time I was a little tired and admittedly a bit snippy when I said, "I imagine the liquid comes out the front and anything more valuable out the back, pretty much like all dogs." Marlie ignored me and opened the bag and Pepsi dutifully hopped out, squatted, *did his business* and was about to hop back into the bag when a Great Dane approached on a harmless reconnaissance mission. I can only surmise Pepsi had never seen or been that close to a large dog. He startled, gasped, and dropped dead! Not a great afternoon at the park, but thank God it didn't happen on my watch. Of course the upside was that I never actually had to dog-sit the little hairball. RIP.

I was feeling the pain, not of being left at the altar, but by the mad scramble from so many of my friends who appeared to be in a race to get to one, leaving me with far too much time on my hands. I threw myself into work to compensate for not having a life. I loved designing evening gowns as they offered up the most license for creativity, but I had become the go-to designer for my friends' and their friends' wedding dresses and all their bridesmaids' dresses as well, which meant I was often designing one of the bridesmaids' dresses for me. I was up to six by this count and I had worn everything from melon to fuchsia. Unfortunately, my dresses always had to have sleeves or little jackets and they could never be nipped at the waist because I didn't have one, and they couldn't be strapless, as that would require blueprints for a special bra built by a structural engineer. But I dutifully marched down aisle after aisle, carrying bouquets as varied as the brides themselves, from loose to tightly pinched, even a beautiful, almost undetectable fake. I didn't want to become resentful but I was getting a bit too close to that feeling for my own comfort.

And then Vally, who seemed to have gotten married only four minutes ago, had a baby shower for her soon-to-be born twins. Given all the premarital sex she had indulged in, of course she was having multiple births. I was more than a little surprised she wasn't having a litter. I had known most of the girls at the party since they were virgins, meaning I had known them all a long time, but almost simultaneously they all started speaking in foreign tongues: *"We have been looking for our china pattern. It's not easy finding just the right one." "We have decided to stay in school and we'll live with my parents." "We love all the same things." We* want to puke.

I needed my own guy, but so far that had proven impossible. I was considering living with the Massai, but they were too regal. I was more the run of the mill super-size Samoan type. I liked the idea of living on a South Pacific atoll, but the idea of grass skirts and having to go topless nixed that. Maybe I should be hanging with the guys who piloted the Goodyear Blimp—they were already comfortable with my kind of shape. Despite of having loads of friends, I was lonely.

I was so sick of the insatiable fire-breathing food dragon winning. I had to gain the upper hand. I knew how to starve but I didn't know how to eat and I was unable to get off the diet train, convinced that my forty-seven extra pounds was all that stood between me and finding true love. That's what every magazine told me. There was no way I was going to staple my mouth shut—I had far too many opinions desperate to leap from my always moving lips. But the more validation I got from being the funny, fat girl with the exercise show, the more confused I got.

I heard about a new and supposedly fool-proof diet created by an osteopath, Robert Linn. He had written a bestseller called *The Last Chance Diet.* That's exactly how I was feeling. I had one last chance to get this weight off. It was perfect—no food whatsoever—therefore there could be no fudging with amounts or calories and best of all, no exercise was required. What I did on my show was just for show . . . *Oh God, why did I have to use the word fudging? Now all I can think of is maple glazed fudge* . . . The Last Chance Diet plan was simple; it revolved around fasting and then drinking a very tasty concoction that somehow looked and tasted a bit like a drinkable strawberry Jell-O shake that was very filling. The weight melted off as if someone had taken a blowtorch to my ass. I believed I had finally found the right way for me to keep it off.

Nothing fit me anymore and I had to buy new clothes . . . again. I also had to get new underwear, but not granny panties or Kate Smith bras. Instead I got lace, and I intended to show it off, pretty much to anyone who showed any hint of interest. I took validation from jerks and losers, and all they had to do was pretend to like me. The cable guy, more than a little rough around the edges, made the mistake of giving me a free movie package and I was happy to show my appreciation by getting to know *his* package. A drunken neighbor flirted with me, but if I hadn't been there he would have flirted with a doorpost. I was still like the needy retriever that had been without water for far too long. I lapped it all up and lied about my regret the next morning.

"Mirror, Mirror—Is that me? Why do you like me now?" I was the same person I was six months ago, but I wasn't. I had wings but no idea how to use them. Nor did I understand the whirlpool of emotions, the good, the bad, and the ugly that had come with this new territory. I knew I was never going to have a trophy wall of captured boy-heads, so I chased, stalked, and I scored. I knew none of them were playing for keeps but I still reveled in getting their attention, if only for a limited run. There was Roger the engineer who found me amusing. Unfortunately his wife didn't; she found out where I lived and one day I came home and discovered a large knife lying on my bed with a note saying, "Stay away from my husband." I hadn't known he was married. I had the locks changed that day, and I never saw Roger again.

Then there was Brian the art dealer, who dueled relentlessly with me if he thought I was getting more attention that he was. He was *way* too much work. Russell, so cute, so little, I felt like Gargantua whenever we . . . whenever. There was Jacob from Germany; he was bossy but handsome, and at first I thought I could handle his demanding personality but then he insisted I dress only in leather. I looked like a couch. *Auf wiedersehen.* Then came Gordon, handsome, smart, a real candidate until I found out he was a total liar. He tossed out sweet talk as if it were confetti; he had never met anyone as exciting as me . . . I was the funniest, the sexiest . . . I was hooked until I ran across another fish on the same line, who had also been caught with his well-rehearsed spin. Bye-bye Gordon.

I was experiencing a delayed form of sexual adolescence. It felt good to be looked at like that, but I was also angry at any of the men who did the looking and scared by my own out-of-control responses. Why couldn't they see me before?

I was exhausted. I felt drained and depleted. I couldn't suck back one more of those shakes. Hungry again, I fell from the wagon with a thud, eating caramel popcorn, laced with chocolate sauce. Depression and failure oozed through me. I began calling random numbers from my phone book desperately seeking a real connection and just as I hung up from a dead-end call, the phone rang. It was a new friend, Dave, a newscaster from the TV station, saying that the Jamaica Tourist Board was doing some cross promotion and had offered a trip for a bunch of the personalities; best of all it was *free*. He thought it would be great if I joined them. The timing was miraculous. I don't think Dave could quite understand the level of my gratitude.

I begged and made promises to my mother that I'd make up the time by working weekends when I got back. She was happy for me but was worried that my father was going off the deep end. He had taken to standing at the bus stop with no real plans to get on any of them, but carrying a pad and pencil so that he could take notes. If there was a puddle and the bus splashed him, he wrote a letter. If he was standing there and they didn't stop exactly at the right spot, he'd get that bus's number and dash off another missive. My father wrote the most articulate but damning letters ever, citing times, street names, and their coordinates and when he could get his binoculars focused in time, he got badges. If he had left me just the money he spent on postage in those years, I could have gone to Paris and back, twice.

I was in Jamaica on a paid holiday just because I did backbends on TV. I was amazed by this unexpected gift of good fortune. That was the upside. The downside, and there were a few, was being on a yacht with a group of mostly beautiful bikini-wearing creatures. Dave had neglected to mention that the girls who were coming along were mostly product models. They were all lovely people but they were gorgeous. I realized I was there to be comic relief; every moment of this adventure was being filmed by the Tourist Board for future airings and a guaranteed humiliation for me. Why did I set myself up? Somewhere in the blind spot of my brain, I had deluded myself into believing I would look just as gorgeous: my long blonde hair blowing back from my face as I sat long-legged on the prow of the rented sailboat. Instead, I watched the skin on my short and somewhat stumpy legs turn from white, to fire red, to dangerously blotchy as I sat huddled in a corner near the back of the boat. *Yes, I was wearing sunscreen!* I was becoming overwhelmingly queasy, but it didn't matter because the gorgeous ones—all the others—had moved up onto the prow and were sipping pastel-colored cocktails with hibiscus flowers in them. I heard the tinkling of glasses and tinkling of laughter. But I was facedown on a bench, desperate to be ignored—no problem there. I was seasick, my matted hair plastered to my clammy face. I felt the camera swooping in for a close-up. I was in no condition to render the cameraman unconscious. I simply succumbed to the embarrassment.

For me it seemed like days later, not hours, when we glided into a slip and everyone hopped off the boat. I hauled myself to my feet and prayed that a rogue wave would sweep me out to sea. No such luck. They had all gone off to cliff dive or ride some G-4 rapids. I was on the beach, happy to be alone and off that damn boat. I was minding my own business, which is not allowed when one is fat. It's everyone's business. A beautiful redhead jogged past me wearing a pink string-thing just as I knocked back a slurp from an equally pink Pepto-Bismol bottle and admitted through my queasiness to having the fleeting, okay lingering, thought that if I looked like her, I'd just be wearing earrings. She turned around and began running back toward me. Had I just created a fantasy moment that she and I would body bump, then split apart and both our bodies would be perfect? I knew it was a fantasy but she stopped right in front of me and her big blue eyes gazed into mine . . . *No way! Was she hitting on me?* Don't go there, there's no way, but then her hand gently touched mine. I was really confused. In a soft voice, she introduced herself as Melissa, and then said she hoped I wouldn't be offended. Immediately I tensed up, knowing that somehow I was going to be, "You have a really pretty face and I like to help people." *Oh Jesus—here it comes:* "I work for the Ayds Candy Company and we have these amazing appetite suppressants. They come in chocolate, chocolate-mint, and yummy butterscotch. They will absolutely kill your appetite. Awesome huh? I'll give you some samples . . ."

In that instant my seasickness vanished, replaced by a wave of rage, "What makes you think my body is any of your business?" Her face crumpled into confusion.

"Don't you want to be thin and beautiful?" Yes, but I wasn't going to tell her that. I did my best to gather up my shattered dignity as I walked away and prayed for quicksand.

The rest of the trip proved to be just as humiliating. The whole group was going to Dunn's River Falls, a natural wonder that thousands of tourists loved to climb. I felt the wave of fear hit my stomach. I didn't like to climb anything. I didn't want to be a poor sport, so I gamely splashed a smile on my face as I joined the throng of vibrantly dressed pilgrims. In front of me was a tour group of seniors, already itching to take their arthritic legs on the big climb to the summit. The sound of the rushing water, the squealing kids and adults, was doing nothing to calm my escalating tension. My group was already hop-skipping and gloating their way to the top. I was on my own. I took in a deep breath, ignoring the warning symptoms of constriction in my rapidly tightening throat. My palms, now sweaty with fear, should have been the second tip off, even if my stone-like legs being welded to the flat rock I was standing on were not. It was like being on a freeway at rush hour with anxious, honking drivers closing in on me. "Could you go a little faster?" I couldn't go at all. I was stuck literally between a rock and a hard place. I felt the impatient line becoming hostile. I lifted one leg, then the other. I didn't look up and I couldn't look down. Like a fat snail, I slowly inched forward. They were breathing down my neck and it was only making things worse. I didn't respond well to pressure. If my legs had let me, I would have jumped! No flight or fight was to be had here, just a mass of quivering jelly glued to a rock, halfway from the top and halfway from the bottom. I wondered if my mail could be delivered here, because this was now where I lived. A pushy mother of three toddlers yelled at me to, "MOVE!" Another angry voice told me that I was holding up the line.

I was ready to cry but instead I snapped: "There shouldn't be a line! We are in the middle of a freaking natural wonder." I took a few panicked staccato breaths and pushed forward another five steps. Why was I so terrified? I stopped and clutched an outcropping of rocks to let the never-ending parade of climbers squeeze past me on their journey upward, as an equally long parade made their way back down—like a busy colony of nonstop worker ants programmed to carry their trail mixes to the top, and their empty cellophane bags back down. I was paralyzed. I was stuck. *Oh, a metaphor . . .* For a microsecond my neck unfroze, and I looked up to see my party of bikinied wonders all staring down at me. Warm pity flooded their faces. A park ranger appeared at my side like Gandhi. He put one arm around me and pulled me close, so I couldn't really see in front of me. He gently and firmly guided me down from the ledge, softly talking me through each step.

When we got down to the bottom, the wild applause competed with the volume from the rushing falls. Were they clapping because the obstruction was off the mountain, or because they were genuinely happy to see the concrete melt from my feet? It didn't matter, I was just so grateful to be at sea level. I promised myself to commit to memory that it was my imagination that was agile, not my feet. It was then I saw my new archenemy; the persistent cameraman had captured every second of my personal hell on film.

The makeup department on my show was not happy with me when I got home. They had to slap a primer over my peeling skin, somewhat like a plaster base, to smooth out the bumps before they could apply my makeup. My guest speaker that day was a renowned endocrinologist. He was there to talk about metabolism and I was hoping he'd tell me mine was slow and therefore give me a pass on my weight. He didn't. He basically told me to move more and eat less. *Thank you. Tell me something I don't know.* Shockingly, he did. I told him I had been doing The Last Chance Diet. Immediately, a stricken look crossed his face and he made it clear that he hoped

I was no longer messing around with something so nutritionally unsound and dangerous. He told me, the yummy strawberry shake was made of ground animal byproducts like hooves, tendons, and horns and that of the some 2 to 4 million people that had tried the diet, at least fifty-eight had suffered heart attacks while on it.

Once over my shock, I finished the show putting extra effort into my knee squats and bicycle kicks as if to ward off any impending evil, or the possible damage I might have brought on myself while on the diet from hell.

13

Not Always a Picnic

Diet #17 ✦ **Life's a Picnic**

Cost ✦ **$350.00**

Weight lost ✦ **11 pounds**

Weight gained ✦ **Couldn't even look**

A fter the last monstrous diet insanity, and the three before that, I vowed to be more sensible and do as the endocrinologist had advised; just eat less and exercise more. A normal person would have simply made a weekly grocery list and gone to the market, coming home with healthy food and nothing else. I went to the market armed with my list and my best intentions but then I arrived at the freezer section where there were several new items: from easy-heat cream cheese and apple blintzes to Sara Lee's whole section of mouthwatering desserts. I grabbed a couple with the intention of having just one nibble a night. Ninety-six dollars later I was lugging bags through my front door. I had all the healthy options, but deep down in the bags, well hidden, hopefully from myself, were the high-calorie goodies. These weren't really impulse buys, they were necessities in case my mother had a flip-out over my father's worsening condition, or for any of life's unexpected beat-downs. Some people build fallout shelters, some keep earthquake provisions in the trunks of their cars; in my case, the refrigerator was my escape hatch, stocked with all the emergency rations a person could need to ward off most demons. But what was my problem? I really needed to understand *why* food was my touchstone. I came from a good, if somewhat crazy, family—*doesn't everyone?* I had great friends and I had a couple of great careers going on. I had some troubles—*doesn't everyone?* I had an appetite. I'm not talking Hannibal Lecter here, but in this world, having any kind of appetite is considered a crime.

It dawned on me that should I ever get an urge to commit a real crime, like hold up a bank, the picture on the bank's grainy surveillance camera might actually be recognizable. Hundreds of squirrely-faced, bank-robbing nobodies could get away with satchels of money, but even if I had a stocking mask over my face I'd still be made: "Large-size woman lumbering, looks like she's got queen-size support hose on her head." I know even a geriatric security guard would be able to take me down. I hate running, everything bangs and bounces. Worst-case scenario: the guard might shoot me and then I'd make the eleven o' clock news. My family would see the humongous chalk outline where my body once lay, and they'd know instantly that it was me.

I still hadn't answered my question. Why was food my go-to? Could it be some kind of peer pressure thing? Was I unconsciously rebelling against the power of the media, always pushing perfection on every magazine cover, billboard, television commercial. Was I really that insecure, that shallow? I didn't want to believe it but . . . yes! Who would I be if I had been gifted with a great body? A pole-dancer? An exhibitionist? It was impossible to know because I was filtering it through my *wanna-be* brain. Or was it that I was weak? Lacking in willpower. How often had I heard; "Get a grip and push away from the table." It might have been wiser for me to stuff my ears instead of my body. A win-win; I wouldn't be able to hear the haters and really, they wouldn't be there if I knew how to push away from the table. Too much thinking was making me hungry.

I had enough girlfriends to know that even the near perfect ones only saw their flaws, magnified as if they could be seen from space. "Oh my God, look at my ass—It's huge." Every mirror was Judas. It lied and betrayed, showing everything through a distorted prism. I knew intellectually when my friends looked at me, as when I looked at them, we saw our personalities, our hearts, and our souls. But still when we looked at ourselves, we saw only fat! I could see Katja, with her perfect body, look at herself and see that she hated her thighs. She kept pulling her sweater down over them. My sister, also blessed with a great figure, fixated on her little tummy pooch with complete disgust. In her eyes, it was a giant jelly-bellied monster! Why were we so hard on ourselves? Why did it matter if we were

a bit thick around the middle as long as we were not thick in the
head? Why did we care so much if we had a double chin? Or had
less than perfect arms? Why did we all want to be line drawings?

Imperfection is beauty
Madness is genius
And it's better to be absolutely ridiculous,
Than absolutely boring.

—Marilyn Monroe

I decided if a gorgeous woman like Marilyn thought that, then I
needed to do a better job with my thoughts. I stopped dieting and
tried living. That lasted two and a half months—just long enough to
eat my way through my emergency supplies, restock, and do it again.

Fate intervened in the way of another potential job. I was summoned to meet a charismatic character by the name of Chris Bearde,
a producer who was in town from Los Angeles. He was looking for
someone with personality and humor to be a regular on the *Bobby
Vinton Show* for CBS. We immediately hit it off and I was hired to
begin the following month.

I did what I always did. I immediately went looking for a new
and better diet, one that was not crazy. I scoured every newspaper
and magazine until I found a diet tacked up on my local supermarket
billboard; "The Life's a Picnic Diet" consisted of three meals and two
snacks delivered to your door. If I never had to enter a kitchen or a
restaurant, if those places were made obsolete, maybe then I would be
fine. No danger zones. No temptation. But much like room service,

diet delivery meals didn't come cheap. Apparently you needed to have a million dollars lying around, so that some person could deliver three teeny weeny, perfectly balanced feasts in specially designed, reusable miniature picnic baskets. I sold an heirloom cameo in 22 karat gold just to afford that picnic. (I had precious few of those, so it had better work.) Of course, I would need money to stay in the "Life's a Picnic" world, lots of money; either I'd have to inherit it, marry it, or make it myself, and since all of the above were unlikely, I would have to go into debt, or learn to cook.

Three weeks later, I arrived at my dressing room for my new TV job, feeling pretty proud of my eleven pounds lost and more than a little self-righteous until I saw my costume. It was a brightly colored and heavily padded dirndl with an oversized puffy-sleeved blouse and an opera singer's Wagnerian Valkyrie helmet attached with fake blonde pigtails. In my excitement, I clearly hadn't listened to the entire job description. It was my job to escort the featured guest star onstage by way of a polka. The celebrity *du jour* would then, reading from the cue cards, hurl a fat joke or insult at me. I twirled Don Rickles to his mark, center stage. He looked me over, "Hey kid, what did you do, swallow a stove?" I was devastated. They had hired me only because I was fat! I lasted a season and a half. After the first season, I quit, but CBS wanted the show just as it was. The producer made promises that this time it would be different. They didn't know what a terrific comedienne I was when they hired me. They wooed and cajoled and I fell for it. I was naive and inexperienced in the big, self-serving world of show biz. Oh, they gave me sketches to do; when Phyllis Diller couldn't show up, I got to do her sketches but they wanted them delivered exactly the way Phyllis would have done them and even back then Phyllis was old. I was a girl in my twenties, and I still had to polka out the guest stars and endure their cheap shots at my expense. I didn't care if I ever worked in that medium again, so their threats fell on my deaf ears and I quit for the second time. This time they really were unable to convince me to return. They offered it to John Candy. He turned them down. I should have done my homework; Chris Bearde was the man who created *The Gong Show*.

From then on, I was far more conscientious about what jobs I would take and I swore to never again be the butt of anyone's joke.

14

Retreat

Diet #18 ✦ **A week at the spa**

Cost ✦ **$1,450.00 (not including the flight)**

Weight lost ✦ **5 pounds**

Weight gained ✦ **1.5 pounds, and it's only midweek**

True love remained elusive. With every pound I lost or gained, I seemed to lose me even more, especially after I bumped into Ben. You may remember him, he was the boy who wouldn't have sex with me in the backseat of that ill-fated car when I had the loopy idea that I needed to lose my virginity in order to lose my baby fat. My feelings got hurt when he rejected me; our friendship fizzled and we never really got it back on track. Neither of us was mature enough to make that necessary first move.

When we accidently met again, we spent an awkward couple of minutes making stilted small talk until we sat down in a coffee shop and fifteen minutes later we were solidly back in the groove of sharing gossip and secrets. A long time had passed since high school and there was much to catch up on. Ben was unhappily working for his dad, managing the family sportswear logo factory, something he swore he would never do. He was divorced after a two-year marriage and he felt his life had crashed and burned. He was depressed. He was lonely. He was surprised to hear that I, too, was depressed, and that I felt I had one foot nailed to the floor while I spun in the same circles as I had always done. He told me he was impressed that I was doing so well and how much he enjoyed my antics on the exercise show.

After sharing a pizza, too much wine, and an anxiety attack, we fell into bed. WOW! Ben was shocked. I was shocked. Ben and I began spending all our time together. It was easy and familiar. I began to think Ben was the one. . . . We spent nearly every night together for a couple of months, but it gradually occurred to me that we never went anywhere. We never left my bedroom. There were no ball games, no movies, and next to no restaurants. I pointed this out to him. "You're crazy; of course we go out," he replied.

I smiled, "Great, let's go out now!" I could see in his face, something was up. Of course, that made me insist even more. Ben defended his position by telling me he was just happy to be ensconced in our own world, but I wasn't buying it.

He leapt up, "Fine. Let's go to a movie."

I didn't even know what the movie was, other than it sucked, but that turned out to be the best part of the evening. We were just leaving the theater when a group of Ben's college pals swarmed him with joy. He was equally thrilled to see them. I stood to the side waiting for him to introduce me but the introduction never came. It seemed like ten minutes of high-fiving, back-slapping, and catching up. It was like I wasn't even there. I realized he was embarrassed—that I wasn't the person he thought he was supposed to be with. All the tension and feelings of discrimination bubbled up to the surface like boiling lava desperate to blow. "Take your shame and shove it!" I kissed him full on his lips. "Explain that to your buddies." Bye-bye Ben.

I was almost out the front door of the theater when Ben caught up to me. He was blazing mad. He grabbed me by my arm and confronted me. "You want to believe the worst. Is it possible that you got that picture wrong?" He said those guys were on an opposing college team and he didn't remember their names. He continued lambasting me saying that I had self-esteem issues and I wanted to blame the universe for what he never thought was my problem: my weight. He went on to say that I embraced being a victim because it made me right and everyone else wrong. I was dumbfounded into total silence by this last remark. I was filled with righteous indignation, hellbent on getting far enough away from Ben to think about what he had said and to lick my wounds.

I chose to plug my ears and my mind and go about my life, just as I always had, not wanting to believe that what he said might be true. Once again, Ben and I were on the outs.

I needed some TLC fast; I had no idea what that meant but I knew I needed it. I was talking to one of my closest friends, Karen, who suggested we go away to a spa. It sounded very fancy, but I was in desperate need of a break from being me so I didn't care what it cost and, in little more than the time it took to toss some workout wear plus a couple of bathing suits and half a dozen head-to-toe cover-ups into a suitcase, I was airport bound. Karen was sweet, kind, pretty, and petite, so why on earth was I going away with her? We boarded the plane and I took my seat. I reached for the seatbelt with a slight beat of trepidation, but breathed a sigh of relief and a moment of pleasure when I realized whoever had been in that chair before me was quite a bit larger than I was. I couldn't have asked for a better start to our trip.

The spa, "El Rancho Del Porko," as I liked to call it, was set in a beautiful but arid part of Mexico and a world away from Toronto. A gentle and caring guide wearing a sarong and more than a hint of patchouli took us on a tour of the grounds and the facilities. It was a beautiful setting with pools, meditation gardens, and yoga studios—indoors and outdoors—and pretty wooden huts in the woods where they held the exercise classes. She then invited us into the dining room where all the newbies gathered to have tea and be given a rundown of the week's offerings. Soft, hypnotic chimes played as we sipped our apricot infused green tea and ate delicious fruit and waferlike cookies. This was going to be good.

Karen and I shared a room, which was simply decorated and beautifully tiled and outfitted with the softest towels and organic shampoos. We were excited to wake up and dive into a week of wellness.

Those huts in the woods that I had admired were really boot camps designed to kill. I tried to keep pace with the bellowed instructions, blasted over the blaring hip-hop music, but to do so, I was in need of an iron lung. These were militaristic exercises run by an ex-Navy Seal (I was sure of it) posing as a braided, sweet flower child, and she had riled up the spandex-wearing women into an aggressive frenzy. So much for the gentle chimes; these broads just needed some spears and hunting rifles and us slower-moving endomorphs would have been roasted on a spit for that night's dinner. I was pretty sure if those loud tunes were played backward and in slow motion, one would be able to hear threatening commands: "Right leg up—NOW! Left leg—NOW! March faster! DIE! DIE! DIE!"

A daily siesta was what I had planned on doing with my afternoons. Not bloody likely . . . There were endless hills that had to be climbed and I was rousted from my slumber by some gung-ho, trailblazing maniac who wanted me to understand this was part of my journey to well-being. She assured me that I would love the fresh, *dry* air, and I would love the endorphin release I would feel when we got back from our two-hour butt-burning hike.

Seven minutes in, I determined that dragging my fat ass up those desert hills was sure to result in my death if I even attempted to keep up. My whining began, "I hate climbing; I am always last. I *hate* this. I *really* hate this!" Caterpillars must have heard all my wheezing, bitching, and lumbering eighty miles away. And I was horribly and desperately thirsty from sucking back all that sand. But like Dumbo, I believed I could somehow do this. Oh crap, Dumbo was a really bad metaphor. I was at one with the program, rising at dawn to begin the healing, the shedding, and the rebirthing. Seriously? I prayed the squadron of trainers could help me get a grip.

Three days later, I was no happier about climbing those damn hills, and our insanely chipper leader was grating on my nerves; she even whistled while she walked. Karen was complaining about not being able to lose the five pounds that seemed to stick to her like glue. I snappishly told her that it was called skin and she needed it to keep her organs in place. Gung-ho Gal overheard me threaten Karen that I would "shove her skinny ass into a sharp cactus if she didn't shut up." The condescending, holier-than-thou leader stopped the entire yoga-pants-wearing parade of speed-walking, tanned, and seriously toned overachievers to lecture me that Karen's five pounds were her cross to bear. Still huffing and puffing, I pointed out that I was carrying the entire weight of the world, which was a wee bit heavier than a cross. Apparently, I touched a nerve as the whole lot of them ganged up on me, believing that I had not just attacked their religion but their bogus chubby-assed issues as well. It was not a good start to my day.

It went rapidly uphill from there when one of the spa Gurus or Goddesses, I'm not sure which they preferred, began dinner with an incantation: "Do what you have always done and you will get what you always got." My internal voice belched to the surface, "Okay, don't eat so much, can't you just say that? What's this costing me?" It was decided I had an attitude problem. "Yes, it's true. I'm hungry!" The yummy, organic locally grown lettuce wraps weren't doing it for me.

I tried harder and I hiked the blistering hills, muttering sailor-like filth to myself. I swam endless laps, did stretches at sunset, and ate only whole grains and holy blessed leaves. I visualized me as I was intended but somehow the picture of the long-limbed, sun-bronzed me wouldn't hold. It kept sliding back into sun-blotched, potato-woman. But the massages, the good-for-you food, and even the hard-core workouts had absolutely had a positive effect on my psyche and on my body, and being with someone as supportive and good-natured as Karen had all helped me to better my attitude—or so I thought.

One night, a talking stick was passed around and we were to share our body issues. "I hate mine. Next." We each tied a ribbon onto the stick with our special wish written on it; of course I was given a stern look when I wished for "lasagna." As the evening progressed, everyone used the opportunity to pour their hearts out about what emotional hot buttons triggered them to eat, to drink, or to inflict bad behavior on themselves or toward people they loved. There were tears and laughter, too. There was a sense that release could be had just by being honest. But I sat with my arms folded tightly around me, not sure why I couldn't or wouldn't share my pain or grief or whatever the hell it was that was keeping me stuck. It was so deeply buried that it scared me, so I made jokes, believing that entertaining the troops was my contribution. I was surprised to see that was not what was wanted from me. But it was all I had to offer.

Things went from bad to worse as I acted out like a bratty seven-year-old child, but how I enjoyed every minute of my rebellion. I was paying for this spa—or in this case, a fat camp—but no longer wished to be here, not because it was too hard, but really because it wasn't what I expected. I had wanted a mindless escape with some pampering and a light amount of fitness and health training but instead I was at a gulag that not only wanted me to burn off the pounds, but also wanted me to bare and share my soul in public. Not happening. Ultimately I found my people, the few Teflon-coated black sheep who also resisted the cajoling, prodding, and pushing to march to a beat that we couldn't quite follow.

But then I was busted for stealing grapefruits from one of the trees right outside my room. "They're grapefruits for God sakes! Not cupcakes!" My emergency stash of candy was found in the toe of my hiking boot by a tattletale maid—please don't tell me she was cleaning my shoes.

I was called on the magic carpet to stand trial before the Goddess-in-Chief, who was worried I might stage a coup. I could only imagine that if I *were* to stage a coup, it would involve butter, sugar, and flour. I was given the speech: "You continue to do what you have always done and you *will* get what you always got." I threw caution to the wind and said, "I hope that means ice cream." I was banished from the spa. I was disruptive and my attitude was toxic to those who were serious about cleansing themselves of bad habits. I felt released, but not in the way the Spa Gods had intended. I felt comfortable with my decision not to be bullied into *feeling*.

I arrived home to an answering machine full of messages. Five of them were from my mother and several were from my agent to tell me he got me a national commercial. Of course he didn't tell me that I would be wearing a hot-pink leotard and most of the shots would be focused on my leather-strapped derriere, being jiggled and shaken, as I stood on one of those ridiculous vibrating machines, all shot in a very tight and supposedly funny close-up. What this had to do with Scotch tape was beyond me. By the end of the fifteen-hour day, my rear end was quivering all on its own, and I was yet again feeling demeaned.

I had hoped to come home and drown my sorrows in a nice hot bubble bath while scarfing down a large bowl of anything with cheese, then climb into bed wearing my favorite flannel nightie, but once again the answering machine was full with calls from my mother. I shut the machine off along with the rest of my crappy day.

I woke up full of sinner's remorse. "I will only eat greens today, maybe a little chicken, skinless, and I will drink gallons of water until I flush the evil toxins from my body and mind, and I will hit the treadmill and power walk until I am once again worthy. I will. I will.... Maybe just a teeny bit of bacon, a bite of sausage, with a side of hash browns, crispy ..." I turned the phone back on and played back the messages. My mother's first message sounded tired and fed up but by the time I got to the last one, she had unraveled and was not making much sense. What I did hear was, she was at her wit's end and couldn't take another minute of my father's crazy behavior. I called back but there was no answer. I tried again half an hour later. Still no answer. I panicked and grabbed the keys to my car. What if something had happened and he was in the hospital—or worse?

So much for not feeling; it was not possible.

15

Throwing in the Towel

Cost ✦ **No one cares**

Weight lost ✦ **Seriously?**

Weight gained ✦ **Yes!**

I couldn't understand where my parents were. I had checked with the hospital and my father's doctor, and thankfully he was not in either place; yet neither of them was home. They never went anywhere together! My curiosity was further piqued when I saw a newspaper lying open to a heavily ringed, red-circled ad for used cars. I could feel the agitation pinging from it. Neither of them drove. It didn't make sense. I heard a taxi screech to a halt in front of their house. My mother bolted out of the cab and stormed inside, hauling a suitcase behind her, followed by my very confused father. The front door slammed.

Seeing me sitting at the kitchen table, her shoulders slumped down in release at having someone who might understand. "He is old, like parchment, and he needs to be in a home where he can have proper care. Yesterday, he walked to the bus stop in his pajamas and he wasn't going anywhere. He had his paper and pencil and stood there taking names and numbers until Mrs. Soumis from down the street got him to come back home. I can't do it anymore! I'm not young either." She grabbed the newspaper and waved it in my face. My father had still not made it into the house. Her finger stabbed at the circled ad: "Old Volks Home." She was more amped up than usual, explaining her eyesight was not what it used to be. She had seen the words "Old" and "Volks" and called the number and asked the man who answered, if they took old *volks*? He said they did, so she packed my father's bag and called a taxi. I had begun to feel something like panic mixed with incredulity sweep over me as she continued, "When we arrived at the address from the phone book, it was a used car dealership, not a home for old volks. Volkswagens! *Aaach!*"

I was fighting to keep from spinning out of control on so many fronts. That she had tried to take my father to be warehoused in an old-age home without talking to me, and probably without discussing it with him, either, was bad enough, but that she had taken him to a used car dealer was awful. My mother's Austro/Hungarian accent somehow extended to reading as well. She was always mixing up her V's and F's but this was too crazy. "You took Daddy to live in a used car dealership?" Despite the absolute sadness attached to this misbegotten adventure, I fell apart, hysterical with laughter, which

infuriated my mother even more. But then she, too, recognized the insanity of what she had done and collapsed in laughter right alongside me.

My father walked into the kitchen and took in the unusual picture of his wife and daughter gasping for breath as we laughed until tears were pouring from our eyes. "Well, that was a rather odd outing." His understatement only set us off again. He continued, "I think a cup of . . . a cup of . . . of . . . what is it that I want?" My father was losing it at an alarming rate. All his years of half-life had become his reality. A vat of ice cream injected directly into my veins would have been good right at that moment.

So began our Sunday-in-the-country drives to find my father a home. My mother and I sat in the front and my dad sat in the back, lost in his own head, counting the many uses for corn as we drove by one full field after another. "Corn . . . corn . . . oh yes, more corn . . . What do they do with all that bloody corn? I suppose cornflakes, corn chowder, corn bread, corn fritters . . . oh, cream of corn . . . right, right, oh corn dogs, very strange indeed . . . popcorn!"

We passed one pretty Victorian mansion after another; very few were still private homes, but there were quite a few that had become funeral parlors. I'm guessing they sent a message of stately calm and serenity. A few were now bed and breakfast establishments, but the majority, it seemed, had been transformed into elegant looking retirement homes. There were peacocks in front of one, Harbor House, a retirement community; a pond in front of another, Winston Manor, home for the aged. We pulled up in front of several of them, hoping

to see a sign from my dad that he responded to one of them more than the others. He seemed oblivious but I believed he was in denial.

We parked in front of a particularly appealing red brick mansion, The Folger Home, and went inside. It was just like all the others. The entryways were warm and welcoming but the farther in you went, there were no peacocks, just rows of pigeons in pajamas, all waiting but they didn't remember for what. They were sitting in large waiting rooms devoid of life, waiting for the end of theirs. Reading from the brochure, Queen Elizabeth was doing the hard sell: "A place to care for your elderly in the way you would care ..." I hoped not, but it was a done deal, and I sent her home in a taxi. I didn't want her to get him settled, as I knew he would be forever unsettled with her overcompensating presence.

"It looks nice here. They serve tea in the lounge at four every afternoon, just like in England." I was chirping, my voice was becoming higher and higher. "They have chess and backgammon, and I saw some people painting. I think you might like that. There are a couple of nice looking men your age ..." Of course they were his age. I was babbling like an idiot. He was quieter than usual as I unpacked his suitcase. It had so little in it: a few well-worn sweaters, a pair of nice grey pleated trousers, a couple of pairs of pajamas, a McDonald tartan bathrobe, and his favorite slippers. There were no dress shoes but he wouldn't need them. "I've packed your favorite books and a brand-new atlas with big print. I know how you like to roam the world. There's a bag of soft caramels. I have a feeling once you settle in, you'll be quite happy not to have to hear Mummy's nagging and

I wouldn't be surprised if there were a couple of single ladies, just waiting to chat you up."

The stillness shrouding him was like a thick impenetrable fog and I couldn't shut up as I tried to pierce through. I looked at him to make sure he was breathing. He was standing so still. I could barely breathe. This was his last stop; he knew it and I knew it. I helped him to sit but his body was stiff like stale saltwater taffy. I had to help him unbend, one wrong move and I worried a piece of him would snap off. I touched his arm . . . I wanted him to know . . . I don't know *what* I wanted him to know. I understood his fear. He softly reached up and patted my hand. I was supposed to be reassuring him, not the other way around. I wanted the blood in his legs to pump and I wanted him to run. A friendly Filipino male nurse arrived to check his vitals. I kissed my father and bolted from the room. I felt like a traitor.

The director of The Folger Home asked me to step into her office to discuss my father's care and other pertinent issues. After answering my questions she pulled a sheaf of papers from her desk that I needed to sign. She wanted to know who to notify in the event of death. "Is there a Mrs. Parker?"

A hard brittle voice leapt from my throat, "No, there isn't. You call me. Is he going to be okay?"

She draped her arm comfortingly around me as she walked me through the lobby to the front door. "He'll be just fine. It's like a cruise ship with lots of people in the same boat . . ."

The stresses and strains had begun to take their toll on me and I wasn't sleeping well. I was uncharacteristically moody and unable

to focus on work, but work was the one thing that calmed me. I put my heart and soul into designing a line of blouses, skirts, pants, and dresses that would look good on us Chubinskis. It was sexy and playful, but still classy, managing to cover the parts us big girls wanted and needed to conceal, but made the most of what was intended to be on display. And none of it was black. It was vibrant, feminine and pretty and I called the line, Full Bloom. My sketchbook was almost full, but instead of taking it to a manufacturer to have the samples made, I put it away along with my ambition to be the Coco Chanel of fat fashion. I wasn't in any condition to take the leap. My addiction escalated, manifesting in a wholesale slaughter of anything resembling food. With every bite I got angrier and angrier but I didn't know at what or whom, so I turned it inward. With my father now firmly in a home, my mother had finally abdicated any pretense of her bogus marriage and I understood I was now solely responsible for his life. I couldn't breathe and I kept my hands deep inside my pockets so the shaking wouldn't be visible, even to me.

Every day I drove to the old peoples' warehouse and I sat in the parking lot looking up at the gray windows, looking to see if I could catch a glimpse of the gray man I had abandoned there. I saw only slow moving shadows. I would take a deep breath, suck it up and head inside. But on this day, doing what I always did, I took a deep breath and lifted the door handle to get out, but my legs were cemented to the floor. I knew I was supposed to get out of the car and go in with a smile on my face but I couldn't do it. I left, squealing my tires as I bolted from the parking lot.

I called my close friend Arlene. I needed someone safe to sit across a table from while I ate to stuff down my feelings. An unsettled storm was brewing, moving in on me. I was fidgety and irritable and couldn't even concentrate on the menu. "I'll have the chicken. You must have some kind of chicken. I don't care if it's battered or bruised, just any kind of chicken. Thank you." Arlene looked at me, trying to see how she could help. She had barely uttered a full, concerned syllable when I slammed her hard. "I'm fine!" I apologized and excused myself. I had to go back. Arlene squeezed my hand in gentle understanding and I handed her a bunch of bills, which she wouldn't take. I told her I would call her later and I was out the door. This was my father. What was I thinking? He had already been abandoned by my mother.

The elevator doors opened and I stepped out into a cuckoo's nest of vacant-eyed, scrawny pigeons all sitting in their wheelchairs, waiting. I walked right past my father. He, too, was sitting in the waiting row—death row. He was wearing mismatched pajamas and a three-day stubble and no teeth, the man two wheelchairs away was wearing *his* McDonald tartan robe. I found his teeth in a glass next to his bed and gave him back his smile. As I released the brake on his wheelchair to take him to the cafeteria, all the pigeons looked up at me with pleading eyes, begging me to take them, too. They lurched forward, trying to squeeze onto the elevator but the doors began to close as the man wearing my father's bathrobe jammed his wheelchair in the gap. The alarm bells went off. He stared at me in defiance, refusing to budge. I needed to know the penalty for killing someone already on death row. A pair of orderlies came and

pried him loose but by then my father had lost interest. I returned him to his room.

Oh God, my heart just skipped. It skipped a beat. I got in my car and I drove home. I was having an out-of-body experience. I was driving but I was sweating. Who did these people used to be? They had lives; they were me. They used to answer phones, pay bills, kiss and be indignant over stolen parking spots. Now they were shriveled and diminished, just bits and bites of memory, bursts of rage, and endless hours of nothingness.

Somehow the car arrived in its parking place. Somehow I was in my house, dressing for a dinner. The powder puff in my hand was damp. Oh my God, it did it again. I felt my heart skip, as if I'd hit an air pocket. My throat was closing. Was this a heart attack? My legs were numb. I was becoming paralyzed. Was this some deadly strain of spinal meningitis? Or a deadly bacteria? What did I eat? What did I eat? I was going to die. I wanted to call for help but my mouth opened and my voice wouldn't come out. My brain was stuttering. I couldn't breathe.

Somehow I made it to my neighbor John's door. He immediately sat me down; asked me nothing. I could see in his face that he knew I was in trouble. I needed to tell him what was happening to me, but I couldn't speak. What was happening to me? This made no sense. The air pocket hit again. WHAM! My heart dropped into my stomach. I was terrified. I looked at John. He picked up my hand and stroked it rhythmically, back and forth, alternating with a different rhythm ... pat ... pat ... pat ... stroke, stroke. If I could have moved, I would have smacked him. My breath was back. "STOP

THAT!" John breathed a sigh of relief, realizing I was okay. I was definitely not okay but I could speak. What the hell just happened to me? Oh God. I was embarrassed. I was scared.

My brother-in-law, the doctor, diagnosed me as having had a classic anxiety attack. At least it was a classic: timeless and always in vogue. He prescribed Valium. I took one and immediately dropped anything that came into my grasp. I didn't want to be *that* relaxed. But I wanted the Valium; I wanted them by my side just in case. I put them in the glove compartment, in pockets, drawers, shoes—everywhere. But the attacks didn't come. I lay awake at night, testing the demons, conjuring the most horrible of thoughts. Nothing. Had they gone, or were they lying in wait?

I watched as my father steadily dissolved, like ice cubes melting into nothingness. I wanted to save him. I wanted to bring him home, but I didn't have enough room and I had stairs. He needed special care. He needed diapers for God sakes! I was a bad person. I didn't have the Mother Teresa gene; I got the Eva Braun gene—something definitely passed down from my mother. It wasn't my fault she didn't want him. Of course, she *never* wanted him but he was mine now. He should have prepared for his old age! I didn't even know him. I had to go back and spend more time with him. I had so many questions and so few answers . . . There was so little time.

I walked quickly through the lobby of The Folger Home. *No eye contact. No eye contact.* I plucked my father from the row of pigeons. I kept my head down and I didn't open my mouth until we were seated at a table in the florescent, overly lit cafeteria. I was babbling in hyper-drive. "How are the books? Tea? Do you want a scone? A

nice dessert would be nice. Would you like that?" He didn't answer me. He just stared at his reflection in the window, seeing nothing. I put a donut in his hand. "So are they treating you alright? Have you made any friends?" Oh God, I was talking to him like he was a child after the first week of summer camp. I felt my breath start to quicken. This man wearing mismatched pajamas was my father and I had no idea who he was. And now I was scared there wasn't going to be time to find out. I don't think we'd ever had a real conversation. Please don't let it be too late. Who are you? Were you ever in love? Have you had any happiness in your life? He took a bite of the donut not hearing anything I'd said. He didn't know when his mouth was full and kept adding more. I watched mesmerized, looking at the conveyor belt; his hand to mouth, donut in one side, a sodden piece dropping from the other. In, out, in, out until there was a pile of mush on the table in front of him.

He patted his mouth, smiled, and pulled on my sleeve. "All done, very nice . . . very nice indeed. Nurse, could you take me . . . *uhm* . . . back to my house now. I have to . . . I have . . . " I nodded yes. I looked at my father and saw nothing. There was nothing to see. Pirates had come in the night and stolen all his treasure.

Why would I have wanted to be on a diet? I needed padding to keep me out of the nut house. What I really needed was pudding. Pudding was better. I wanted to climb inside a vat of it and either drown or be the super woman I knew myself to be and eat my way out of it. There were those who would condemn me for falling back into my comfort zone of food but I didn't care. I don't judge those who drink too much, snort too much, sleep around too much,

organize their clothes on color-coordinated hangers—whatever it takes to get them to the other side of a difficult and thorny patch of life—I take my hat off to them. As long as the only person they're hurting is themselves. It's better than jumping off a bridge, leaving a mess for others to clean up. The only bad part about being a secret eater is that it isn't possible to remain one, as my pain-relieving ways showed themselves soon enough.

16

Falling Rocks

Diet #19 ✦ **The Baby Food Diet**

Cost ✦ **$24.00**

Weight lost ✦ **4 baby-sized pounds**

Weight gained ✦ **7 jumbo-sized pounds**

My father was parked on a side rail, rusty and no longer of any use. The Folger Home was doing its best to keep him entertained and comfortable, which was not always easy seeing as he was convinced he was back in merry old England and that the beleaguered caregivers who looked after him were family members whom he had never trusted. He was *still* keeping a list and taking names, along with all their infractions. To ward off my ongoing fear that Ms. High Anxiety might make an uninvited appearance, I still kept some Valium in the candy dish at home, which was empty of candy because I had eaten all of it. Not that I was ever planning to take the Valium, but I needed to know it was there. It had become my security blanket.

I had never thought of myself as a depressed person, but my recent behavior said otherwise. I had always thought of myself as outgoing, happy, and a self-starter. Perhaps I was like Sybil, that oft-written about multiple personality. Maybe I had a different persona for every occasion and Rotunda, the dark one, had eaten me out of house and home.

Whatever the truth, I knew I never wanted to be thought of as a victim. That's not who I was. I was the cheerleader and the instigator of fun.

My mother's boutique dress shop catered to a very privileged and demanding clientele, and she was their much sought after queen. I had taken to the role of princess as comfortably as ice cream on cake; the clients liked me and my mother was proud, sometimes too proud, and misguided. Whenever I lost ten pounds or more, she'd look at me and say: "You could be a model." I would look at her and tell her she needed a white cup and a cane, as clearly her vision was gone or the mother filter was so rose-colored it blocked sanity. I had come to the conclusion that most Jewish mothers thought their daughters looked like Audrey Hepburn, even if they were sporting duck lips. Going to work every day was like picking my way through a minefield in a pretty garden. I loved my job, but my mother was my boss and her lifelong mixed messages had me spinning, the general theme being, "You are perfect just as you are, but a few changes couldn't hurt." That, coupled with her ease at setting my father adrift in an un-swimmable sea, deeply upset me.

My inner Southern girl had come out with a vengeance, cooking carbs as if I were a female Paul Prudhomme on a bender. I devoured crumbly, toasted mac and cheese made with butter, a little more butter, triple cream Paradiso cheese, and a hearty thump of sharp cheddar, fried chicken, and anything au gratin. Once again, I had determinedly thrown myself off the wagon. All modeling requests, even from those wearing tinted lenses, ceased.

I buried myself in my work, designing everything from luxurious coats to wedding dresses. I loved the embroidered silks, the floaty chiffons, the boiled wools, the textured weaves; I loved them all with the same reverence I had when I encountered my first jumbo box of Crayola crayons. The colors made me swoon with possibility. I didn't have the same reverence for the clients; they were often demanding and difficult. My mother's one-of-a-kind, handmade, custom-fitted dresses and gowns took weeks, making sure the designs suited the bodies that would wear them, with precision fittings, attention to detail, and the awful reality that all that labor would never pay off as most of her customers could never understand the concept of time is money. My mother always paid her dressmakers, her suppliers, and her rent. There was never much left for her, and when her customers pushed and wheedled until she knocked off a few more dollars, she just sucked it up and gave in, her old world ways winning out. I simmered and swore I would never take over her business no matter how much I loved dreaming and drawing those dresses. I was sick of being poor and pretending to be rich—that was my mother's specialty. I knew I needed a more lucrative, but somehow also creative career, as I wasn't cut out for the world of high finance. My exercise show was fun and had brought me lots of attention but it was a small cable station and the pay was barely enough to keep me in the fancy chocolate I loved.

I had stumbled into my new passion, writing and performing, by telling tales about my fractured family; they were the gift that kept on giving. I couldn't keep my mouth shut, much like a spewing volcano with a need to erupt. I was funny on paper, funny in person, I was even funny alone in my bathroom. People began to notice and I was in demand as a writer! And as an actress! I had found my G-spot and was being paid for doing what I had always done, amusing myself at my own expense. But I couldn't just walk out on my mother's business, especially when things were so fragile. My father got worse and my mother, always hovering on the verge of bankruptcy yet still pretending, was taking out loans she would never be able to pay back. So I stayed.

When I was young, I remember going on a family bus trip to visit what seemed like hundreds of castles in the highlands of Scotland. In the pass, high above the craggy rocks, I read a sign that has always stuck in my head: "Watch for falling rocks." Life is like that; we're supposed to watch out for falling rocks but it's not possible. We cannot stand guard waiting for bad things to happen. Rocks fall when rocks fall. I tried to tough out the panic attacks, which were now coming with the regularity of a Tokyo to Kyoto bullet train but I was sure that my sweaty palms, shortness of breath, and the brand-spanking-new fear of highway driving were glitches brought on by being a bad daughter; if I would just visit my father more, if I could forgive my mother for dumping him, they'd fade away. Of course one was easy, the other would require a much-dreaded, head-on confrontation. I chose the Scarlet O'Hara option and put them both away for another day. My anxiety attacks escalated and my comedy career stalled.

My wonderful friends, led by my best and heart-stoppingly handsome gay pal Stephen, decided it was time for an intervention, and just as I was locking up the shop they descended, armed with a giant picnic basket filled with everything from shrimp quesadillas to champagne and a boom box. Stephen, true to his tribe, also brought hats, wigs, and plenty of sparkle, believing it was time to cheer me up. Eating in the shop was *verboten*—fear of stains splattering wedding gowns—but in my current condition I didn't care, seeing as food worked way better than tranquilizers. I marshaled a small army to make sure everything was covered in plastic and let the music rip. I was instantly made over into the high priestess of a gaggle of store mannequins that were placed in a variety of positions at my feet—some worshipful, some more risqué. It felt so good to laugh. The transformation from sad girl to my joyful self was made complete by being tended to with so much love and a whack of silliness. I would have married Stephen then and there if not for the struggle we would have had over which one of us would wear the wedding dress . . . and the teeny issue of a life of celibacy.

A couple of loud and funny hours later, someone complained about the noise; the police arrived just as one of the store mannequins, dressed in not much more than a bridal veil, was being danced about the shop in a conga line of blond-wigged men dressed as women. Despite looking like a fat Barbie in drag with punky nails, giant blonde wig, and a magenta boa, I believed I carried off a fairly respectable version of myself. I apologized profusely to the officer, explaining this was a bridal shower for a girl who had been very ill and had just woken from a six-month coma after not being expected to live. It was such a stupid lie but I'd had a lot of champagne. Somehow the officer went with it and left, passing on his best wishes to the bride and whichever "girl" she was marrying.

Small victory. I was more terrified that my mother would get wind of the mayhem so I asked everyone to pull the shop together and leave; the half-naked mannequin, the boys, and everything else disappeared in minutes.

About a week later a terrible odor began to emanate from the shop. First we searched the various trash receptacles for rotting lunch leftovers but found nothing; next, cleaners scoured the place from floor to ceiling but still the smell remained. Clients began to notice and, as though they were visiting medieval France, they quickly reached for perfumed handkerchiefs or their sleeves to protect their wrinkled noses from the offending odor. It was embarrassing and not ideal for hosting fancy customers, so we called in the fumigators—the consensus being there must be a dead rodent in the walls—but they, too, found nothing. The stench got really horrible and I was sent out to neighboring boutiques to see if they were suffering the same fate; perhaps it was a sewage problem. Nothing . . . My mother was contemplating calling a Realtor when I made the gruesome discovery. I was redoing the window display and found the party mannequin, which had been shoved into a back closet along with the other castaways. When I pulled off one of her arms to get a dress over her head I almost keeled over from toxic shock. I covered my nose and mouth before pulling a plastic bag filled with a furry, greenish, former seafood offering. Someone, in his haste to clean up, had shoved it into one of the arm sockets. Wishing I was wearing a full hazmat head-to-toe covering, I scurried to the farthest outdoor garbage bin in the back alley and tossed the foul-smelling evidence, slamming the lid behind me as I gulped for clean-smelling air. I was destined to be done in by food even when it was nowhere near my mouth.

On a sad and sobering visit to see my father in his less-than-glamorous setting, I discovered he had no idea that he wasn't at home and, worse, he wasn't quite sure who I was. As I was leaving, a frizzy, too blonde octogenarian in a motorized wheelchair blocked my path to the lobby door. She threatened me with a pointed finger, demanding I stay away from her husband. I promised I would, once I found out which one he was.

I was done and done in, overcome with the realization that my dad was near the end of his life without ever having really lived this one. Silently, I said a prayer for him and then one for me, determined this would not be my fate. I wanted there to be big, noisy footprints to follow in my wake; I had no idea at this point what that meant but I knew it was a solid gold requirement, along with finding love. I had no idea how to go about fulfilling that plan either. Did I have a pheromone on the fritz? I had become a magnet for beautiful, unattainable gay men, and singularly awful and disinterested straight men. My self-esteem had completely plummeted; what was I putting out there? I was brain-ranting, never a good thing when food is one's go-to stress buster—one more nail in my plus-sized coffin.

I needed to get away, someplace where I could get some perspective. Montreal was only a few hundred kilometers away, but there must have once been an ancient ocean between it and Toronto; it was French, need I say more? Every woman there knew how to tie and twist a scarf; even the homeless beggar women looked better than I did. It was a revelation to see how effortless it was for French women to embrace their own style. I vowed to shake off the couture restrictions my mother lived by and become more fully myself. But first, I needed to soothe my wounded soul. I took refuge in Atwater Market, a food lover's paradise. The cheese counters brimmed with hard and creamy blues and Bries so ripe they oozed. Braided and twisted breads covered in nuts and seeds were piled mountain high, and pastry vendors beckoned with layer cakes, chocolate mousse cakes drizzled with white and rich dark chocolate ganache, and custard oozing out of everything else. I filled two shopping bags and checked into the first hotel I bumped into.

I was in full pity-party mode; pity I was alone, pity I had the appetite of a walrus, pity I had no self-control, and pity the maid who had to clean up the trays, candy wrappers, and my fat-ass carcass because I planned on dying here. A few hours later I woke up from my food coma . . . hungry! How could I be hungry? I had just eaten enough food to lift a small Third World country out of its misery.

But there I stood at the doorway of a crowded café looking for an open table, when a hawklike woman looked me over and shook her head. I was terrified she was going to shout, "Av you not 'ad enough?" I kept my head down and found a table in the corner; the sound of chairs scraping, plates clanging, and all the fast, French-talking, alien babble was weirdly soothing.

I was immersed in the origami-mess of trying to make my scarf look nonchalant and fabulous when this way-too-good-looking French guy interrupted by asking if there was room at my table for him. I would rather have been impaled on a church spire. I wanted to be left alone but nodded. My scarf was now knotted like a noose. He introduced himself as Gilles. Apparently he was the chatty type. I mumbled my name, which he instantly Frenchified, "Ah, Monique." I had had enough of pretty men; I stood up, grabbed my coat, and prepared to leave, rattling on about all the important things I needed to accomplish in the next hour or two: buying socks, washing my hair, promising to be in a police line-up and judging a shwarma-shaving competition.

He thought I was funny, he thought I was charming, and he said something about, "The snow being big balls now and how I must sit for the time." I thought he was hilarious, even though I'm not sure what he said exactly or why I listened but I sat back down. His English was terrible, my French worse, but the day turned into evening and we were still talking; maybe I was talking, maybe I was dreaming. He wanted to show me "ees Montreal."

I ventured into the slushy night with this beautiful English-challenged man, wearing a pair of ridiculous platform shoes that I had no idea how to walk in, but thankfully, he hailed a cab and I stepped forward onto the frozen pavement . . . and immediately slipped right onto my rear, one leg under the taxi, the other splayed off to the side. Embarrassed, I pretended it was a party trick, claiming it was a specialty of mine. Gilles picked me up; I knew I had twisted my ankle and it hurt, much like my pride. He offered to take me to my hotel. I was horrified; my room looked like the aftermath of a nuclear holocaust. I was too embarrassed to even let room service see it but I couldn't walk so I nodded. Somehow we arrived and I threw a blanket over the mountain of food entrails that he, for some reason, appeared not to notice. Of course, he was blind! That's why he was here with me! But then, this man got ice for my foot, ordered tea from room service, and picked up everything, saying, "You resting, I will make the dinner, yes? I am make for you the bath and then you be refresh and *voila* then we will have the eating."

I found myself lying in the bathtub going over everything he had said, not understanding most of it, and wondering why I felt okay about being in a bathtub, naked—I guess that was the only way to have a bath—even with a total stranger in my hotel room. What did he mean, he would "make the dinner?" There were no dishes and certainly no stove but still my eyes closed in relaxation. Then, "did he send me off to have a bath so that he could rob me? Was this some pervert scam? No one was that nice ..." Oh my God! He was coming in. I grabbed a towel—shit, it was a face cloth. I tried to cover ... what? One boob? One knee? He said something about needing, "ze showere cap." Had he come in to get a shower cap or to kill me? And then he was gone. In shock, I got out of the tub and wrapped myself in the biggest towel, a little late, shook out my hair, pulled on my clothes and limped out of the bathroom.

There were flowers in an ice bucket and a salad in the shower cap; there were candles, two hotel place settings, and crystal stemware. Gilles explained, as if this were normal, "I have go to ze store for the baguette and ze things: prosciutto, a beautiful cheese and fresh figs, and a whole chicken. I take ze elevator for every floor and I pick up from the tray what we need. The flowers are from ze lobby. We will put some back maybe later. You will sit."

I couldn't eat. I had no appetite and I pushed food around on my plate as if I were an anorexic. What was happening? We finished dinner and he sat me on the bed. Momentary panic washed over me until this amazing man picked up my swollen foot in his hands and began to massage it but stopped immediately when he saw me wince. He got some ice from the ice bucket and grabbed a napkin, and bandaged my ankle and foot. He tucked me into my bed, kissed me on my forehead, and he was gone. Shit! He's gay.

I woke up with a huge pillow crease across my face and my hair plastered to my head, as the key turned in the lock. I leapt back into bed thinking it was housekeeping, but Gilles stepped into the room carrying fresh croissants and two steaming *café au laits*. This man was unbelievable.

The day passed in a haze; somehow we never ran out of things to say. At a café we both noticed an old man who gave up his seat so a pregnant woman could sit and who was then rewarded by two ladies inviting him to sit at their table. He flirted with both of them—an arrangement that made them all happy. Store windows, passersby, and a shape-challenged construction crew struggling to fit a manhole cover back into place elicited mutual conversation and laughter, even though we could barely understand each other.

It was night when we returned to the hotel. At this point, I could no longer afford it, but I had no intention of checking out of that enchanted castle. We were in the hotel ballroom, and there was no one around when Gilles sat at the grand piano and began to play. Of course he could play. The teeny tiny ballet dancer that had always lived inside me quickly shaved her legs and strapped on a pair of toe shoes. I stretched out my long slender arms and arched my back. I was a swan and I *jeté'd* across the floor, on my toes—leaping, limping, twirling. I was a feather and I swanned across the room toward the piano. Momentarily I caught my reflection in one of the gilt mirrors. I was an ox—a fool. Gilles asked me why I stopped. He looked at me and suggested I was perhaps scared. I leapt into denial, "I don't know what you're talking about. I'm not scared of anything! Well, I'm scared of edges and bugs, all kinds, and . . ." He had my face in his hands and was looking at me, really looking at me.

"You are scare from something. You say it to me, then, it will not be so big, it will be outside of you and maybe inside me, my problem, not yours, eh *voila*. Okay?" It wasn't okay. I was terrified of getting hurt but he said that that was out of our hands. He couldn't make promises, but we needed to take the chance, *c'est la vie*. I looked into his beautiful, ocean green eyes and saw nothing: no lies, no bullshit. I needed a little bullshit, but there was none there. I felt the bars around my heart pull away and I kissed Gilles as hard as an ox in toe shoes could.

I manufactured another trip to Montreal under the guise of having been made an interesting designing offer. I had to have more time with this man. I needed the time to convince him that I was the one. And if that failed, I was willing to resort to kidnapping and hobbling him until he got it. I have no idea what he was drinking but he didn't seem to need my threats. He was as into me as I was into him. That was worrisome. *Why?*

I had a boyfriend, maybe, but he lived 365 miles away. My phone bills were in another galaxy. I didn't care. Fiddle-dee-dee, he was coming to spend the weekend with me and I bought new sheets. Seriously, I bought a whole new bed, but what if he didn't come? Shut up, he's coming; my brain was fuzzy from the lack of food. I hadn't eaten in days. I wouldn't have thought five teeny jars of baby food a day could be considered food, and yet some enterprising hustler had just come out with The Baby Food Diet, promising yet again that the weight would slide off while still providing the body with all the nutrition it needed. Yeah, if you were a baby! But I went for it, praying all those little jars would make me little. All I had to do was eat a complete breakfast; rice and bananas, just add water. For lunch, applesauce and sweet potatoes. And for dinner, turkey and vegetables with prunes for dessert. I could even have snacks. I was a 175-pound baby, sucking back jar after jar of pureed everything. I began to develop a retrograde crankiness and fussiness with an acute need to be rocked, possibly institutionalized. I desperately wanted to be erased, redrawn better, thinner.

We hadn't "done it" yet but in the hopes that it could happen, I replaced all the light bulbs with dimmers. Maybe he *was* gay or worse—maybe he was a hermaphrodite. Again, he just walked through the door, no knocking and no warning. Thank God I had slept on my back, in my makeup. I was beyond nervous, having moved directly to fluster, "You're here. You're early—twelve hours early! I mean . . . hi. *Mi casa, su casa* . . . Wait, you're not Spanish, you're French . . . bonjour." He had brought me flowers but then said he thought he should have brought me tranquilizers. I had had enough of those. After we shared a bottle or two of wine—he had one glass—I was calm, a kind of drunken calm. It was as if we'd been together forever, and he was not gay. He was amazing. I prayed that what had just happened between us was not a figment of my parched imagination.

I had always hated Sundays. Everybody always had plans while I read books. Gilles and I were going for a walk in the park and I loved this Sunday. He was holding my hand and I was holding his, admittedly in a blood-drawing clench, but after a while I loosened my grip a little and he was still there. It was beautiful and I was happy until I felt something on the periphery and my body tensed up with a deeply embedded sixth sense. Warning! Danger!

A group of teenagers were hanging about a huge oak tree, smoking, and missile-firing acorns at each other. My radar was pinging loudly. I tried to steer Gilles in another direction but he was oblivious. One of them yelled, "Hey Friar Tuck! You want us to get you a turkey leg? Hey Fat Stuff!" I was shaking. I couldn't control myself and I began to shout, "Shut up! Shut up! You ruined it! You're ruining it!"

Gilles stroked my arm, attempting to reassure me that they were just a bunch of stupid kids showing off for one another. He couldn't understand why I was so upset. How could he not? In a barely audible voice, I explained, "Because, now you know . . . you know . . . you know I'm fat." Gilles gently assured me that he already knew this. He told me he liked me just as I was. I immediately called him a chubby chaser. I think he had no idea what that meant, but he did know it was some kind of accusation and he looked deep into my eyes.

I thought I saw a golden halo appearing just above his head as he softly spoke, "I like you, but it is you who don't like yourself. This is your problem and for this you must decide: to accept you as you are, or change, but not for me, for you." Who *was* this man? Did I just see him levitate? Okay, I must have eaten something (not a stretch), and now I really *was* hallucinating.

I decided to close my eyes and leap. What was the worst that could happen? So many nauseating thoughts began to collide; I blocked them out as quickly as they came.

Our relationship flourished in the two train stations where and whenever we reunited, and from a distance I was fairly sure we looked like post-war lovers from a bygone era as we ran into each other's arms, but on closer inspection, I'm sure it appeared as if a tall handsome man was being dry-humped by his long-lost Saint Bernard.

17

In~Security

Diet #20 ✦ **Cottage cheese, celery, and diuretic tea**

Cost ✦ **Pennies**

Weight lost ✦ **Not enough**

Weight gained ✦ **None**

We had astronomical phone bills. We talked and talked, and when it was time to hang up, I was the Goddess of Good-byes. I could drag them out, even resorting to Pig-Latin, anything to keep Gilles on the phone. For several weeks, I existed on a starvation regime of one or two spoonfuls of cottage cheese accompanied by a few stalks of crunchy but totally boring celery—just enough to keep my charm-offensive from collapsing but not too much for my body to keep shrinking. Soon I began my whimpering campaign, "Think how much money we'd save if one of us were to move to the other's city. If you moved here to my house, which is far nicer because it has that womanly touch . . ." My brain was whirring at full speed to find one more selling point. None was needed. To my shock, he said, "Okay."

Presto, chango! Gilles and I began to live together, and I began to fall apart. All my internal strategists were on high alert. In order to survive, they had to contribute ideas or they were going to be bounced from the all-you-could-eat buffet of brain-crazy I provided. One of the voices told me to be funny, another said be sexy. I fired that one on the spot. Be yourself, came from another department; I fired that one too. Wasn't that exactly what I was trying to avoid? It had never worked for me before, but then one of the voices assured me this man was different, that he liked me for who I was. That made no sense. Clearly, he must be damaged goods; it just didn't show on the outside. But there he was . . .

A gargantuan, monstrous, insatiable hunger swept over me. I had a boyfriend, but I didn't really believe it. No matter how much this beautiful man did or said to make me feel secure, I was pre-conditioned to believe that I wasn't the girl who got the guy; I was the girl who wore the big pink butt-bow bridesmaid dress. I was the girl who didn't get asked to the prom. I was going to wreck this; I could feel it and I needed to fill the hole before I got any nuttier.

Why couldn't I have been like Sleeping Beauty and go to bed fat only to emerge weeks later sallow, wan, thin, ethereal. It wasn't in the cards. I ate when I was happy. I ate when I was sad. I fed a cold, I fed a fever, I fed—period! I was Dracula in search of cheese, chocolate, bread . . . I tore apart the kitchen in search of anything edible, preferably not moldy, but in a pinch I could always scrape. Still, the hunger grew. "Gilles do you love me?" I felt this falling from my lips like crumbs in search of a napkin. He shook his head patiently, as if talking to a very young child, saying that everyone told me they loved me; it was the price of admission. It was like this liquid soap; it pours out so easily but it is nothing but bubbles.

"I do more; I show you. The actions, more important than the words . . . *oui?*" I didn't understand why I couldn't have both show *and* tell.

He must have really loved me because I kept coming up with more and more hoops, some of them lit with white-hot fire, but he jumped through them and stayed. I was insatiable, wanting, needing proof of his fealty. Once, he happened to leave his passport on the dresser and I hid it, thinking he wouldn't ever be able to leave me. I know, *insane,* but when he went looking for it, I never said a word. It was my insurance policy. I was on overdrive trying to appear casually comfortable rather than my clingy mosslike self around everyone who ventured into his path. I wanted him to like my friends but when he did, I felt threatened, possessive, panicked, unhinged—all of which I knew enough to mask with a ridiculous representation of faux-graciousness.

At a girlfriend's birthday party filled with gorgeous young up-and-comers, I was standing by the buffet just to test my willpower. It was a game I knew I'd fail. I was really standing there to give me a place to casually survey the room—okay—to keep an eye on Gilles without appearing Velcro-like and possessive, which I was but didn't want him to know. I watched as a very beautiful, tall, feline hung all over him as if he were her personal scratching post. I reached for the cheese tray. A few minutes later she slithered her way over to me and picked a grape from my fully loaded plate, popped it into her vixen-red mouth, and hissed, "What did you do to get him?" I felt sucker-punched. I desperately wanted to make a sharp and funny comeback but my mouth was full. I caught Gilles' eye and we connected. I knew then and there I wouldn't need to knock the teeth out of her vicious, lipsticked mouth.

But the crazy-train kept coming. One magical winter's day with snow gently swirling as it fell, Gilles and I had plans to go skating. He clearly didn't know my history with blades, but my heart was willing even if I doubted the body would get the memo. We made our way hand in hand to the subway; he held mine in a gesture of affection and I held his so as to stay upright on the icy sidewalk—so happy, so surreal that this was my life, and not some lie I made up to impress some crap-guy who had hurt me in the past. Gilles dropped my token into the turnstile and I went through. He looked down at his hand, "I have dropped my glove. I will come back." And he was gone . . .

Fifteen minutes passed and I began developing a heart-pounding case of flop sweat. Did he just pay for me to stand on this side of this little gateway so he could run home and pack his things to go back to Montreal? He'd made a mistake and he didn't know how to tell me because he knew I would wig out just like I was doing right then. The teeny seed of doubt was growing and soon it would become a strangling trumpet vine. I couldn't breathe . . . I needed to lie down but where? The concrete was wet and cold, and the parade of people double-wrapped in Gor-Tex and wool kept rushing by and I would be trampled to death—but that might be the best thing. Suddenly, Gilles, with a triumphant grin on his face, hopped over the turnstile, waving his ice-caked glove. I smiled, sweetly; *Oh my God, he didn't leave me.* My face registered only normal. Palpitations and panic were never to be mentioned, sucked back into the vault, as this was a dark moment even for my runaway imagination.

It was right after that teeny panicky episode that I decided to introduce Gilles to my mother. She seemed skeptical when I told her I had met "the one." I responded a touch shrilly, "He's with me because he wants to be, not because he's under house arrest, but because he thinks I'm awesome." I told her I was going to marry him, something I had not yet told Gilles.

She smiled. "I'm happy for you and if you can get him to marry you, don't blow it."

Everyone in my family loved Gilles. I think my mother would have met me at dawn with pistols drawn if she thought that I was ever unkind to him. Gilles laughingly told me she had said if we ever had a fight, and he felt the need to get away from me, she would completely understand. I didn't know why he found that funny. The deck seemed so stacked; I was the one with all the faults and he was painted as some angel plucked down from the heavens to save me. I was riddled with flaws and not too many of them were hidden. I wore them defiantly to see what people were made of. Would they be able to see past the electrified, barb-wire fence?

There had to be something wrong with him. Like a chubby Sherlock Holmes, I sleuthed and surveyed Gilles every moment and I found things, bad things. He was forever forgetting his wallet, his watch, and appointment book, and he was often late. He liked weird food combinations: white bread with molasses and peanut butter, salt on blueberries—small infractions, I grant you, but then I found a biggie. In the kitchen my sweet man turned into Attila the Hun, fierce, warring, territorial, and worst of all insanely messy. It was a revelation and I was thrilled. I kissed him and thanked him, but he had no idea why.

Gilles took me to meet his family who lived in a small town in Northern Quebec. I began knocking back gallons of diuretic tea in the hope that I could pee the fat out of me. It seemed that peeing had become my new hobby. I had time for little else. I had always known we were primarily water but did it all have to thunder out like some break in a flood-zone levy? We had to make pit stops at every gas station and rest stop on the four-hundred mile drive. I thought his family would think I had some bizarre bladder infection. I was a basket case. He laughed and tried to assure me his family wouldn't care whether I was wet or dry, thin, fat, black or white; they'd care about whether I liked his mother's pies, his father's Chrysler. His sisters would care that I liked him and I only cared that they all like me.

It turned out I had nothing to worry about. Gilles' family swarmed about him as if he were the second coming. He was the baby of the family and the only boy. If he was happy with me, that was all they had to know. I spent three days with his family, none of them spoke

English, but they laughed a lot, spun stories, and were as close as my family was not. They never seemed to leave the kitchen table as if it were a special kind of endurance challenge, a.k.a. The Kitchen-table Olympics. It seemed they were there at all hours and, if someone did leave, another appeared to take their place. Many pies were eaten, fortunes were told from a well-worn deck, and I was immediately made to feel one of them. It was easy to understand how my boyfriend came to be so special. *Oh my God, I had a boyfriend . . .*

But I couldn't calm my over-the-top-fear that I would lose him. On the drive home, I casually threw out my most winning pitch: that if we were to get married, it would make our lives far less stressful because I would be so much calmer. He didn't understand why I, who had a mother who could not do this marrying thing well, not once but twice, wanted this so badly. I was too afraid to look at him, but I heard him loud and clear. "Marriage does not make love." I had one last line of reasoning. If he were to marry me, then the whole world would know, well my whole world, would see someone as amazing as he was willing to put it on the line for me, have blood tests and stuff . . . Okay, mostly it would show my mother! The pause that ensued was way too long. I felt my heart was about to be smashed into smithereens. I had my hand on the doorknob ready to leap from the fast-moving car, when Gilles pulled to the side of the road. "I don't really know what it is you have just say, or why it is the whole world that must see. I see, we both do, and that should be enough."

He had no real understanding of why marrying me was so important. He couldn't comprehend why some man wearing a special suit could wave his magic wand and make us more married than he felt we already were. But he loved me and wanted to make me happy; it was the stamped legal paper that sat in a drawer that he objected to. To him it was wrong that that kind of power could be assigned. He looked at me tenderly. "Tell your mother and your friends that we got married in Quebec when we went to visit my family." I think Gilles hoped that going public would satisfy both of our needs. It worked—sort of. I told my mother and, not one to waste the moment, she threw a wedding celebration together, including making an announcement of our nuptials in the newspaper. The backlash from my friends and family, who felt slighted by my not telling them, was overwhelming. In that moment, being a writer came in very handy. I fabricated a story of our spontaneous but perfectly private and romantic wedding ceremony performed by a justice of the peace in a beautiful small town by a lake. I instructed Gilles to fill in all the blanks and forever we were to keep our mouths shut to this lie.

My mother pulled out all the stops. It was a huge gathering, with everyone she had ever known, including our extended family and all of Gilles' and my friends. I had to threaten my over-excited mother to not hire a skywriter to proclaim how lucky I got. My dad wasn't there. He was far too deep in dementia-land. My girlfriends, in an outpouring of gratitude to Gilles for taking me off their hands, all handed him dollar bills. My contingent of former standby dates, my gay posse, did their best not to flirt outrageously with Gilles, whom they all had a crush on, out of respect for my mother. My family plundered their coffers to make my fake wedding special, believing it was definitely cheaper than feeding me for life, which is what I think they thought they were in for. But it worked. I felt married. How could I not? We opened gifts for two hours. I pushed the guilt aside by reminding myself how often I had worn hideous bridesmaid's dresses.

I was lying in bed in that wonderful half awake, half dream-like state, protected from all bad things by *my fake husband's* right arm welding my head to the pillow. I fell asleep again. The phone rang next to my ear. Of course, it had to be my mother who never seemed to understand it was not okay to disturb her newly married daughter early in the morning. *Aaaach!* I wasn't on guard at 8:30 in the morning; a person answers their phone at 8:30 with no trepidation. "Hello? Oh, I see. Yes, I understand. Was it peaceful? Thanks for calling." *Thanks for calling . . .* My precious Gilles put his arms around me. "I have to tell people. Whom do I tell? He didn't have anybody and I already know." My body shuddered with the realization that my father was dead. I sat leaning against Gilles. He lifted the front of his T-shirt to allow me to put my head underneath and lay my cheek against his warm skin but there were no tears. He rocked me back and forth, lulling me into a short-lived sliver of safety. I bolted out in a fury. "I am not telling my mother! Maybe in a year when she thinks to ask, "So, how is he? Your father?" "DEAD! I'll tell him you were asking." I knew I was playing with fire. She'd be mad, but she didn't have that right. I was the one who was angry. She may as well have put a blindfold on him and spun him around three times pushing him in whatever direction she wanted. She never asked him what he wanted. Gilles turned me to face him and softly pointed out my father was more than twenty-one and my mother didn't have a gun to his head. I was adamant about not telling her and about not having a minister. He didn't go to church. I was not having some stranger stand over my father's body and tell the assembled—me—things he was making up about a man he'd never met . . . "Richard Watson Parker lead an extraordinary life . . ." Yeah, he forgot to have one.

My father was not religious. His church could be found amongst the trees and the parks he loved. He had always said he wanted to be cremated so that's what I did. I bought flowers. He loved flowers: lupines, crocuses, and daffodils. We were driving to his favorite park. A car horn blared and I slammed on the brakes. I had no idea why the overcooked blonde in the car next to me was so angry. She swore at me and screamed. I had run a red light. I had no idea. I was on another planet. "I'm sorry. I'm sorry." But it wasn't enough for her. She whipped out from behind and pulled alongside me, rolling down her window, ready for another attack. That was it! I stormed out of the car and was about to get in her face when Gilles pulled me back, but not before I could shout: "My father is in the trunk and he's dead!" With that, she flipped me the bird and was gone. Gilles pointed out she was probably calling the police to report a murder.

I was fairly sure it was illegal to bury your dead in the Toronto Park System. "What if someone sees us? What if we get caught? What if . . ." Gilles calmed me down. "It's okay, we'll tell them, it's our cat Miou-Miou." I pointed out we didn't have a cat, and Gilles countered that we wouldn't miss this one, then.

I found it so odd that the box was heavy. Did that mean that even in death I, too, would be heavy? Life was not fair and apparently death wasn't either. I found the perfect spot, two tall oak trees overlooking a meandering stream. He would have loved it. It was April. It was Canada and the ground was frozen. The digging was arduous, impossible but we managed. I took the seeds out of their packages and tossed them over the newly dug earth. I knew flowers would grow there, and everywhere else the wind blew them. It felt good, simple, quiet, and surrounded by green and trees. I heard whistling—lots of whistling. A long, snaky line of schoolchildren led by their teacher was heading toward us and I felt panic begin to flush across my face. We stood motionless as they stomped close by us, right past the two tall trees, and then they stopped. I watched and saw they were headed to the bathrooms. On the other side of the twin trees where my daddy was now buried, were a pair of red, wooden arrows, one on each tree. One read, "Boys," the other arrow; "Girls." Not quite the marker I would have chosen. But it was an unforgettable one and seeing as I was the only person who needed to know where my dad was buried, it was somehow perfect. There would be an endless parade of little children stomping close to my father's grave and I knew if he could, he would have risen up . . . "Private property! Private property! Go on, have a move on."

We pulled up in front of our house, exhausted, to find my mother standing there, waiting. I opened the car door and then saw she had a knife! It was a butcher's knife and I immediately tried to shut the door but she pulled it open. She was hopping mad like Rumpelstiltskin, going on about having to hear the news from a near stranger. "I hope you are feeling very proud of yourself young lady. ROSE! Rose from the bakery told me he was dead. Not you, but Rose. And she heard it from Liesl, who got it directly from a very knowledgeable woman at a flower market, where you bought some cockamamie English garden for his grave!" I wasn't feeling quite as confident about my plan. I had hit the bull's-eye and it didn't feel good.

"You only care because other people knew before you." The knife blade was suddenly being pointed right at my chest, its gleaming tip milliseconds from drawing blood. "MOM!" She spun the knife around so the blade was now pointed at her chest and thrust the handle into my hand, pounding her chest.

"Go for it. Finish the job you've started." While fighting back relief that she was not going to actually kill me, I marveled at my mother, who deserved an Oscar for her archetypal Jewish mother histrionics. For the first time since hearing that my father had died, I felt the tension drain from my body. I stood before my mother struggling with a mix of hurt and remorse, "I decided you would be the last to know, because I knew it would send you around the bend. I had no idea how angry I was with you." I could feel relief mingled with laughter bubbling to the surface. "And now you have me pointing a knife at your chest."

She was confused by my reaction. "You have a knife pointed at my heart and you are laughing."

I responded, my laughter bordering on hysterical, "Look at you. You figured out a way to make this day be about you, instead of him."

She was holding firm, "He's dead. I'm only halfway there."

"Oh, Mom, you are *too* alive." Of course that made no sense to her. "It's a compliment. Just say thank you and go home. We'll talk about it later. I can't do it now. I need time. I need . . . peace."

I needed a sandwich.

18

The Okay Corral

Diet #21 ✦ **Jenny Craig**

Cost ✦ **$250.00**

Weight lost ✦ **Nothing, I just needed
to pay for it to feel proactive**

Weight gained ✦ **8 pounds**

My mother held fast to her fury at having been the last to know about her husband's death, and continued to give me the ice empress treatment. She told my sister she was disinheriting me. Given the state of her finances, we got a real laugh at her nerve. Whenever I would call her, she'd hang up on me before I could utter a word. I redialed and before she could hang up, I shouted, "Don't hang up on me, you're my mother! You are supposed to be the mature one." She slammed the phone down. I called back again, only to receive a barrage from her wounded pride.

"And you think you are the mature one? *Aaach!* You are now the expert on everything. You are made of stone. You have no feelings. You are just like him! I'm the one who gave *you* life, but what do I know?" The volley took on a competitive life of its own, and she hung up on me again.

My finger spun the rotary dial, "And I know how much you wanted to have me."

"If you're unlucky like me, you get pregnant!" Breathless, I slammed the phone onto the receiver.

Gilles watched this tantrum with more than a bit of concern. "When we have a baby, will it grow up and do this?"

"Not unless you have it with my mother!" I had a small bout of panic. "Do you want a divorce?" He reassured me he didn't but was taking the idea of a vasectomy more seriously.

Soon enough I was parked outside my mother's house loading up on stamina, okay, Twinkies.

I rang the doorbell. Queen Elizabeth wasn't pleased to see me. I apologized for not telling her about Daddy. She stepped back from the door and allowed me to enter.

The vibe was similar to an old Western, but without guns. We didn't need them. We both were upset, and angry, and it oozed out of every pore as we squared off eye to eye in her living room. I admitted that I had wanted to hurt her, but it wasn't planned or even expected. It had bubbled to the surface and then it was just there.

I wanted their hype to be the truth and so I went for a consultation in a slick and very professional looking upstairs lab-like unit in a strip mall. I was weighed and measured and immediately became filled with shame at the results. My very encouraging consultant assured me I would lose ten pounds within two weeks. I took out my checkbook and I felt holy once again.

Two days later, a huge box arrived filled with smaller, attractively packaged and labeled boxes with all kinds of yummy food choices. If only they had tasted as promised. To me, they tasted like dog food, not that I really knew what dog food tasted like but I did know these dishes tasted awful. I would rather have eaten dirt. I went back to tell my consultant but she wasn't there. Another, a clone of the first one, didn't know me and insisted on a weigh-in before I could make my displeasure known. To my surprise, she read from my chart the weight I had started at and magically, and I mean magically, she proclaimed that I had lost nine pounds. For a second I was over the moon, until I reminded myself that I hadn't dieted at all.

It was three months to the day after my father died. Gilles and I were at a retro movie house seeing Steve McQueen in *Bullitt*. It was his favorite, and he wanted to share it with me. We were walking home. "Did you love this movie?"

I had to be honest. "I liked it but I had a little trouble. I couldn't stay with it after his car slammed down that first hill and sideswiped that whole row of vegetable stands. I got obsessed with the mess. Those poor Chinese vendors, all their goods squashed and splattered all over the sidewalk and street. It was upsetting. I worried for the rest of the film about who cleans that stuff up. Messes in movies leave me feeling unsettled; they make me think of my own messes."

Gilles looked at me with affection but, at the same time, he was also shaking his head. "We really are two strangers and you are stranger than anyone."

From halfway down the block I recognized the sound of our phone ringing. My stomach did a sudden triple flip. "Something is wrong."

Gilles remained calm, "Because we have a phone call. You are always think the worst."

My mother had a brain aneurism while playing bridge. She only played competitive bridge—need I say more? The doctor reassuringly explained that any of us could be walking around with a ticking aneurism in our heads and it could live there for years like an unexploded mine, waiting for the slightest wind gust to detonate it. He added that, unlike a stroke, which can turn anyone into a turnip if it's bad enough, a brain aneurism, if found, could be cauterized and the patient would bounce back whole and healthy—that's if it could be found, not easy when it was in the tangle known as our grey matter.

My sister, Gilles, and I paced ceaselessly outside the operating room waiting for news from the front. Oh God, I was desperate for some chocolate, but I knew my timing, no matter how critical, was inappropriate. Heroin would probably have done just as nicely. I watched the door open. The doctor walked toward us, but I already knew, just by the set of his shoulders. Another of life's weird ironies—my mother was dead and it happened while she was playing bridge. Too bad, she was holding a killer hand. But at least she went out doing what she loved.

My sister and I were at the coffin boutique, being shown the bewildering variety of finishes available, from woods of the world, to veneers, brass or bronze fittings . . . *All the better to carry you out with* . . . Discreet little metal pricings stood on top of each customized humidor. I was shocked at the gouging going on, and thinking they probably didn't have seasonal sales or specials. My sister was just as flummoxed. "I have no idea what we should get her. What do you think she'd like?"

That was an easy answer: "A better team of doctors." My sister impaled me with a look. I closed my eyes to fight back the tears and then responded. "The fiberglass ones probably last the longest—I don't know, maybe the walnut? All her end tables were walnut . . ."

We were all having dinner together—my sister, her husband Phil, and all of Mummy's bridge friends. They were all talking about her as if she was still alive. No one had said the "D" word even though tomorrow was the funeral. I asked if they thought Mummy was holding a really bad hand and that was why she checked out. "What do you mean?" I suggested that she had always been a sore loser.

The predictable pile-on was immediate. "Why do you do this? Why do you need to always make jokes?" Easy answer, "The other choice was just too painful." I willed myself into stone and apologized. I kissed my shocked sister and brother. "I don't want to do this dance anymore and I know you won't understand this, but I forgive you." *All their judgments vanquished.* I could see by their faces they had no idea what I was talking about, but it no longer mattered.

My mother was buried with all the pomp and circumstance befitting the Austro-Hungarian Queen Elizabeth. Everyone she ever played cards with was there. Every woman for whom she had sewn beads on bustles came to pay their respects. Her family of seamstresses, her hairdresser, and even Rose, from whom she had bought her bread, came. My mother, unlike my father, had a rich and full life. Speeches were made, anecdotes were shared, but I couldn't say a word. I had just found my mother and now I had lost her.

I left before her casket was lowered into the ground. I looked back and saw a sea of family and friends who were genuinely bereft at her passing. I felt proud to be her daughter.

19

A Fat girl in Thinland

Diet #22 ✦ **The Russian Air Force Diet**

Cost ✦ **1,757.46 rubles or $60.00 per week**

Weight loss ✦ **14 pounds**

Weight gained ✦ **Too much**

W ith both my parents gone, I was not only grieving but I was also out in left field. I loved my mother and father and it was clear that they had loved me, but I was so used to my role as their go-between that, with their absence, I felt cast adrift. The phone didn't ring at all hours with my mother's amped-up rhetoric that she was going to kill my father. She got her wish but my father also got his. It was much like the oft-quoted exchange at a dinner party between the very tart-tongued Lady

Astor and Winston Churchill, whom she loathed:

> *"Winston, if I were your wife, I'd put poison in your coffee."*
> *"Nancy," Churchill replied to the acid-tongued woman, "If I were your husband, I'd drink it."*

I was adjusting to married life and I had very little to complain about. Gilles was not a saint but he did come very close. He cooked, he brought me flowers, and he was teaching me to believe in myself. That was his most difficult challenge; shortcomings were my specialty and I was pretty sure no one would ever demand their money back for false advertising. I kept waiting for the gift wrap to crumble away from Gilles, exposing his true mean and dark underbelly. He didn't have one. I wasn't used to smooth sailing, so I looked for ways to stir up trouble. I would ambush Gilles out of nowhere and over nothing, like demanding to know how he could say he was a Catholic when he never went to church, believed in the right to choose, and didn't believe in Hell. And yet he was bizarrely protective of the Pope. His response to that was simple; it was because he was a Catholic. I challenged him again, accusing him of keeping the door open just in case when he got old and nervous about dying, the club may not let him back in. We went in circles 'til he would declare me the winner, just so we could get back to our far more harmonious ways.

Gilles was a true Renaissance man. He could create and re-create almost anything anyone fancied. He was a phenomenal designer of everything from dresses to drapes and so much more. He could look at anything that someone else had sewn or built and almost immediately know how it was constructed. He would have been an amazing engineer. One minute he'd be salvaging some castaway door and the next it would be sitting in a designer showroom as a much-coveted table, but before you could catch your breath he'd be constructing a replica of an Ottoman-era chair. Amongst our friends, he was nicknamed "MacGyver" for his innate ability to problem-solve. He was not only good with his hands but also with his voice. He carved out a profitable career as the go-to guy for dubbing English films into French. His talents were much in demand.

My performing career had become my true passion and I loved every minute of this unexpected turn. I was hosting a new weekly TV show in which I profiled events happening in and around Toronto. On one episode I was to showcase a comedy club and my producer suggested it would be fun if I were to do a stand-up routine as part of the show. I had no idea how one went about doing stand-up comedy. I was barely an actress and now I was being asked to leap into another alien world. I was terrified. I took to my bed surrounded by balled up wads of paper from endless failed attempts at writing something coherent let alone funny. As my performance night got closer, I got more and more tense and more and more scared. I was almost buried alive under the reams of bad jokes. I finally committed to memory a piece I had written about how different nationalities respond to sex. It was a world tour where some cultures took to it like rabbits, others with acrobatics, and then there were the Brits who preferred to close their eyes, carry on, and hope it would be over before the tea bell rang. I had no idea if it would work but there was no turning back now and I took it all out on Gilles. I was snappish, which only made him and me feel worse. The night came and I felt like I was walking to my execution as I mounted the stage. The bright lights shone in my face and I couldn't see anyone or anything. My knees quaked and I said a prayer. That's all I remember from that moment until I heard screaming fits of laughter and thunderous applause.

Ten minutes after I walked off the stage to hugs and congratulations, two producers who had been sitting in the audience offered me a job writing for a variety show in Los Angeles. At first I thought it was a joke that someone must be playing on me—but it wasn't.

For me the timing was perfect. With the death of my parents, I had no tether; I had shuttered the door on my mother's boutique after coming to understand that without my mother's brilliant dress-making talents, her clients would move on and I didn't want the responsibility of rebuilding the business. My heart just wasn't in it anymore. The TV show only required me once a week and I was at loose ends, with too much time on my hands—and too much food in close range. I didn't want Gilles to have to give up his thriving and artistic career, but in classic Gilles fashion, he believed he could ply his trade anywhere and there would always be open arms waiting to embrace him. I was gob-smacked by his confidence and more than a little envious of it.

When we arrived in California, we moved into Beverly Hills, where we acquired, through a friend, a beautiful sublet apartment we could actually afford. It was not in *the* Beverly Hills, but in the "flats," as everyone who lived in the Hills called them, south of Santa Monica Boulevard, which literally used to have tracks running through them. They were a grand experiment when a vast trolley system called the Pacific Electric "Red Cars" used to run all the way to the beach. Legend has it that the car companies bought the whole thing and dismantled them.

The flats were lovely and filled with million-dollar, red-tiled haciendas on pretty tree-lined streets. They were all considered tear-downs to those *north* of the Boulevard, where the houses had pedigrees and big fat gates and all of the newest owners had a story of a former star or director who had lived there before them: "Lucille Ball used to live here, but the only thing we kept was the upstairs bathroom, which we use as a powder room. Isn't it amazing that anyone thought of this as anything more than a closet, especially a big star like Lucy? Shocking." To live in the *real* Beverly Hills, the houses must come with Hollywood lore. "When Tom was married to Mimi, he lived in the flats, but when he was married to Nicole, he lived up here." *This was all before the Katie years, when he lived in a compound near their BFF's, The Beckham's.*

The question most often asked from a true Beverly Hillser upon being introduced was, "So tell me, are you north or south of the Boulevard? As soon as *south* fell from my lips, the temperature dropped, becoming downright icy. But then I would drop the big one, that we lived in a duplex with three bedrooms and three bathrooms, and we were *renters*. It got worse; we had a two-car garage but we had only one car, and it wasn't a Mercedes or a Beemer, just a car, something nondescript and American. *Eeeew!* With this horrific revelation the frost was instantly gone, replaced by icebergs, and the big-bucks, pouf-headed blondes moved on. We were DOA on so many counts. We didn't belong to a synagogue, a church, a golf club, or a country club, nor did we shop at the *way-more-than-retail*,

Gelson's food-shopping experience. We shopped at normal grocery stores and we always bought the specials and we cooked the food ourselves. There was no maid, no takeout five times a week, just us in the kitchen with pots and oven mitts. Living in Beverly Hills without famous movie star parents or their lawyers as siblings, without a trust fund, or a tattooed and wrinkled rock-star husband, or seriously lipo'd legs and majorly enhanced breasts rendered me socially closer to the endless parade of waxers, weavers, tutors, and trainers that came and went.

Nothing could have prepared me for the strange and beautifully manicured planet known as Beverly Hills, where fat is considered a disease worse than cancer. It is the gathering place for the genetically gifted; a place filled with women who won't be happy until they again reach their original weight—six and a quarter pounds. This is the place that invented size zero. What was I thinking? I was a Martian in comparison to these dames. I hated my floppy jaw and my wattle. It quivered. My arms flapped in the breeze and I refused to look any further down to see the other horrors. I understood that I was a large woman in any town, any city, perhaps, even on every planet, but this is the one I was on.

If money was to be one's report card, in the Hills of Beverly, it was the number one way to be awarded a 4.0. Fame only came in at a 3.8. I was probably pulling in no better than about a 1.3. How was I going to survive? The way I looked at it, I was going to be on life support fiscally and socially unless I could crack the code in a whole new way. I knew I had to take stock of my assets as well as my liabilities, some of which I had already come clean about. I wasn't planning on being rendered unworthy just because someone forgot to leave me a whopping inheritance, or any kind of inheritance, for that matter. Instead I was left a whopping debt portfolio from my mother's overextended business. The irony of being a fancy-ass couturier with a fancy clientele meant the outlay of running her labor-intensive boutique often meant drowning in debt. And dumb blonde that I was, I sabotaged my future by marrying for love and not for money. My sweet husband was an artist not a businessman. After paying off the creditors there was nothing left. My liabilities seemed to far outweigh my assets. I was fat, poor-ish, unconnected, only half-Jewish, and married to a lovely man who was no shark, scion, or rock star.

What was worse, being fat or poor in Beverly Hills? It was a toss-up. Both were considered criminal. Poverty was shocking and alien. There wasn't any. A Beverly Hillser's idea of poor was having only seven pair of Maude Frizon's or only one Chrysler convertible, but I concluded being fat was definitely worse. It smacked of failure on so many fronts. I knew I needed to find a way to gain acceptance. So, if I wasn't going to be able to buy my way in, or bribe anyone, nor offer up any famous parents or famous friends who could open those massive triple-locked Spanish fortress doors behind the many-spiked wrought iron gates, I would need to think of something. My strategy was bold—but it was all I could come up with—I'd have to "embrace" my own failings, make them funny, unthreatening, and hope for the best. Yikes!

It worked . . . not with everyone, but with enough. A whole posse of slim and trim beautiful babes and their very nice, very rich husbands laughed at my confessions and welcomed me with open arms. Not all of these newly formed friendships were destined to last, especially when I had the uncontrollable urges, almost pathological in scope, to not only make fun of me and my *po'girl* situation, but to also poke and stick pins in the spindly but buffed out arms of my kindly benefactors. *Hey, that's what defensive girls with big mouths do.* How could I help myself, when faced with an entire town of women who wanted to look like big-breasted stick figures in heels? To achieve this pinnacle meant never eating again and having the fat, if any could be found, taken from their asses and reassigned to their lips, then lightening and brightening their already blonde heads and adding a shank of Barbie-doll hair to be woven into their own. Sometimes, while walking behind one of the tribe of Michelle or Goldie wanna-be's, I'd feel a pang of jealousy at the sight of these long-limbed, bony-assed babes in their miniskirts and belly-baring fuzzy sweaters, all that blonde hair swinging as they paraded. But then they'd turn around and all my envy would vaporize. Some of these broads were pushing sixty plus! They were all kicking and screaming to stop the clock. No Michelle Pfeiffer; more like Freddie Kruger in *it-girl* drag. I flashed into the future, looking in on the oh-so fabulous "Beverly Hills Home for the Never Aging," and imagined a lot of skinny, smooth-faced old babes with waxy teased blonde sex-kitten do's, sunken mascaraed eyes, bovine-collagen-ed lips and droopy wrinkled bodies, but with perky never-say-die silicone breasts, living out their days. The men, too, would be stapled, with their crop-circle hair implants, saggy, sad, knobby reconstructed knees, and spray-tanned silicone pecs that shone like beacons from their long-gone strutting pasts. There'd be a special wing for those tragic old-fart rockers, with their bilevel and stringy comb-overs, cadaver-esque pumped-up cheeks, and faded tattoos that once read "Mayhem" but were now reworked in the wrinkles of time to say "Mayday." Along this new and alien path I did what I had always done; I made friends. I was just worried I couldn't afford them. Everyone was always private-jetting off to Aspen or Maui or some other exotic posting, where they could meet up with people who looked exactly like they did. Those belonging to the same tribes found each other. It is written . . .

But nothing could have prepared me for this particular dip into the world of trophy wives. Another striking, lean, and long-limbed blonde had taken a liking to me—no doubt she felt so much thinner when in my company—and invited me to her annual "girls only" Christmas party. As a writer, I couldn't resist. It was held at her home, located in a gilded and gated community, where she lived with her decrepit but fabulously wealthy music-agent husband and their adorable brand-new adopted Guatamalan baby. The sun was a scorching eighty-eight degrees, but still an oversized toy train loaded with Tiffany boxes circled a brilliant, iridescent blue Christmas tree standing in the foyer. A kindly but tired Salvadoran woman in a starched white uniform led me out to the pool area . . . *Oh, please not the pool area.* Thank God all the "girls" were wearing cashmere. It was, after all, December. *Did nobody sweat here?* After platters of hot hors d'oeuvres and steaming cups of cocoa with marshmallows were served, which no one ate or drank, we were all given our "Chrissy-prezzies," the Tiffany boxes from the train, which were filled with sterling silver personalized key rings. What the hell were birthdays going to be like?

Gilles and I walked the streets of our new neighborhood as though we had been born and raised by Sheriff Andy of Mayberry as our Pa. Our mouths were always open in either wonder or horror, depending on the moment. On an early morning stroll we were shocked to see how many people wore their bathrobes to walk their dogs. It seemed that not just the dogs marked their territory; every street was considered their owner's backyard. One morning we watched a white Rolls Royce slowly moving up one of the wide back alleyways. We were on a scouting mission to see what priceless goodies had been discarded in the garbage cans. We stepped aside to let the Rolls pass. Peculiarly, the driver's door was slightly ajar and trotting alongside it was a tiny, exhausted Pomeranian wearing a crystal-studded leash, which was being held by the driver as she "walked" her dog. She was an overly teased redhead, her face no longer visible given that it was covered in full-face-lift bandages, making her appear to be Boris Karloff's sister. She stopped at the stop sign and adjusted her mirror, then applied ruby-red lipstick, blotted it, checked her hair—*fabulous!*—and then slowly drove on.

This insanity was soon to be topped by my first visit to my new Beverly Hills dentist. I sat in the waiting room alongside a very pregnant young woman who confided she was there to have her teeth straightened, so her baby would have nice teeth. I was actually out of words. But I thought the possibilities were endless for delusional pregnant mommies; nose jobs for those with hooked honkers instead to be replaced by the more desirable slightly upturned buttons; highlights for the Sephardics, who wanted a better shot for their wee one's cheerleader chances; ribs removed, to give a future daughter a better shot at a beauty pageant title. I could go on—you know I could!

I was guessing the Beverly Hills town council had already moved my case to the top of their pile, desperately seeking a legal way to ban me and my heretic fat-girl ways from ever contaminating the city limits again. But slowly, as I got to know my new surroundings I began to understand that, amid the stereotypes, there were, as everywhere, plenty of wonderful people, and I found them. I did make real friends, lots of them. They were warm and true, and some were ridiculously gorgeous. Lisa, Cheryl, and Barbie took me under their wing, somehow fascinated by me, I thought, much like in the late 1800s when Native Americans were brought across the pond as curiosities to the parlors of wealthy Brits in a form of show-and-tell, only the parlors I was being exhibited in were all in my new town. Cheryl and Barbie were both native Californians, so they knew the strange ways of this alien world and therefore were very helpful in teaching me the unspoken rules. Purses and shoes were far more important than food—they didn't know me very well—but they had to be the *right* purses and shoes. Really, I didn't give a rat's ass about purses and shoes. I didn't feel the need to carry anything else heavy.

They promised to share the secret of Lohman's, where everything was real and could be had for a song, but one had to be careful to make sure whatever you chose was barely out of season. The bigger secret was where to buy the realest fakes for next to nothing, and if worn with the good jewelry, would pass muster even by the meanest eagle eyes. I was very appreciative and they never had to know I preferred pockets to purses, and my feet were far too close to Cinderella's ugly stepsisters' to even contemplate some big-name's dainty slippers. I was given the lesson that Barry Keiselstein Cord was not a man, but a must-have belt. I tried not to laugh. Besides knowing the best $400 collagen-enhancing crème, it was more important to befriend the smooth-as-anaconda-like sales women at Neiman Marcus, who, if they liked you, would alert you when things were going on sale; and if they really took to you, would hide the best merchandise 'til you arrived. Maître d's were the other people who could make or break your day. But a truly excellent tip came from one of the husbands, who told me if I was going to upgrade to a better car, which he seemed to think was a mandatory move if I wanted *any* respect, I should buy it from one of the BH wives. They got new cars almost as often as they bought new shoes, and their trade-in's had no mileage on them, seeing as none of them ever left the protected environs of Beverly Hills.

The best secret I learned was one that I got from the housekeepers I came to know who cared for the beautiful homes in which my new friends lived, and I couldn't wait to share it with Gilles. The night before the giant garbage bins were emptied was trolling time. People in Beverly Hills threw out the most amazing things: brand-new shirts, still in their cellophane or Saks boxes (perhaps the colors were no longer in favor); brand-new Gucci belts that had become tarnished and therefore were useless; high-end vacuum cleaners, tossed because someone didn't understand that the bags needed to be changed and on and on . . . Gilles was the man who could transform the faded and forgotten into the most desirable of treasures. The rest he returned to the shops from whence they came . . . and left with full credit.

Barbie and Cheryl took me to the newest "in" restaurants, their exclusive golf clubs, and the best blond-ers in the world, and everywhere we went there were forests of long legs in tiny skirts, shaking tiny behinds. However, I also met many outstanding women: Nancey, two or three Lisas, Kathy, and Joanna—all warm, all funny, and as good as the girlfriends that I had back home.

But still, I was overcome and feeling the pressure of living surrounded by the "Best in Show." I scanned the checkout counter magazines, inhaling every diet on every cover. I zeroed in on a small ad promoting the Russian Air Force Diet. It seemed to promise the most radical weight loss, and I had long forgotten my mantra about making good food choices instead of picking bad diets. This one consisted mostly of diet sodas and red meat, *lots* of red meat. The models representing the possibilities of eating this way looked toned and fierce; of course, that could have been because they all carried Kalashnikov assault rifles. This turned out to be a very good diet for weight loss, seeing as I wasn't a big fan of red meat. But I did like diet sodas. I could have lost eighty pounds, but I still would have been a water buffalo amid a herd of gazelles. It was pretty clear to me, no matter what I did to fit in, I was always going to be an outsider.

After two and a half weeks I sent the Russian Air Force Diet back to its hangar. My skin had begun to break out and my brain was on strike from drinking too many diet sodas. I was jittery and constantly spaced out. Gilles could not understand my need to willingly jump through these ridiculous hoops. It was hard enough for me to make sense of it, but the desire to be thinner was so deeply encoded in my programming that it had become my default.

Other than that ongoing *mishegas*, we were happy. Clearly in the beginning of some nesting phase, we soon added to our family by getting a dog. It was a very cute and very fluffy puppy, but it was a chow chow and we had not done our homework. They are notorious for being aloof and loyal only to their masters. Gilles and I were both friendly and we liked people, pretty much all of them. Our dog did not. First on her hit list were children, who she hated; second were people of color, who she hated even more. We spent the next eleven years apologizing.

Providence reached out and the ex-pats found us. Los Angeles at that time was apparently Canada's fourth largest city, with well over a million Canadians living far away from the cold. The Canadian Consulate was our home away from home, with their many parties celebrating all things Canadian, from Joni Mitchell to Alex Trebec, Imax, Roots shoes, and whichever films were in contention for winning Oscars. There was, and is, an unbelievable amount of Canadian talent that flourishes among the palms. Our social life quadrupled in a heartbeat with the discovery of many people we had known in the past that we didn't know were also living in L.A. There was immediate recognition of the subtle differences from the Americans that we shared with all other Canadians—mostly our unabashed pride in coming from the home of the Mountie, and our tic of apologizing even if we weren't the ones stepping on someone else's foot. And in spite of having made many new American friends, there was something so comforting in knowing the secret handshake that we Frost-backs shared. For us, the most fun we had was in bringing our two sets of friends together.

We had lived in L.A. for a couple of years when legal issues suddenly reared their heads. I was able to get a green card to continue living and working in the U.S., but Gilles could not, as he was a freelancer and didn't fit the criteria. There was only one answer: to get married. I teased Gilles; it was now my turn to call the shots.

We realized we had a problem on our hands as all of our Toronto family thought we were already married. We decided to not tell anyone back home and just get married at the Santa Monica Courthouse with only a few close friends in attendance. Kim Cattrall, who was a very busy working actress, but not yet the famous doyenne of *Sex and the City* notoriety, was my maid of honor. I had introduced her to her soon-to-be husband and it would soon be *quid pro quo* in the maid-of-honor sweepstakes, only her wedding was to take place on the exclusive shores of the Côte d'Azur. Our ceremony was a surreal experience since I already felt married and blessed, but at least I was no longer a sniveling, whining, emotional hot mess. We couldn't help but feel concerned that everyone back home would find out—and they did. The idea that we could keep our secret was ludicrous. It was too good a nugget of news to stay locked up. Someone told someone, and that someone told someone else, and soon it was a brushfire spreading everywhere until it engulfed our family and friends. Confusion and false memories from people confident they had actually been at our wedding ceremony smacked up against those who were just miffed that they had given us a wedding present for a wedding that never happened.

We decided to follow up our ceremony with an enormous party at our L.A. home, with people spilling inside and out. We asked people not to bring gifts as we didn't need anything and we had friends from Toronto arriving who had already given us a gift for the fake wedding. It was not like any wedding reception I had ever attended. Neither the bride nor the groom were anxious. Our guests were a fantastic combination of Canadians and Americans, mostly in show business and therefore not shy. The food was amazing and mostly made by Gilles. I felt remarkably peaceful and I wanted to make my guests feel just as comfortable, so humor was the daily special, not nerves. Many of my girlfriends took turns wearing my bridal veil, which I got at a thrift store and wore as a joke. It was hard to keep the microphone in any one person's hand for any length of time. People toasted us, made fun of us and everyone else there, and there were great singers on hand to serenade us. It was then that we knew we had made a life in Hollyweird and we were where we belonged.

20

He Cooks, I Eat

Diet #23 ✦ **Fitness equipment and private trainer**

Cost ✦ **$1,100**

Weight lost ✦ **Fat–Yes**

Weight gained ✦ **Muscle–Yes**

I was in love, not just with Gilles, but also with every dish he put in front of me. He was handsome, French, and he could cook. The irony of being married to a man who looked at food as if it was a gift from God was wreaking havoc with my diet-conditioned brain. I wanted to please him, so I ate and I loved every morsel. I wanted to eat the way Gilles did, with gusto and with pleasure, but I was faking it. I had struggled so long with my weight that the soundtrack that continuously played inside my head whenever I ate was turned up to full volume. "You will pay. You are growing as you chew!" Of course, it was unfair that my man could eat three trucker-sized meals a day and then have endless coffee breaks, always accompanied by some sugary treat. He must have a cheetah's metabolism; I, on the other hand, have a garden slug's.

The thing I loved best about Gilles, and there were so many qualities to choose from, was something we had in common. We both loved to celebrate: any holiday, anybody's birthday, any occasion. When we passed each other on a bathroom break in the middle of the night, it presented as an opportunity to twirl each other in an impromptu dance before returning to bed to dream. We shared great joy in making every event special and unique.

One Valentine's Day weekend we were housesitting for friends who had a temperamental dog that was only happy in his own surroundings. The house was a rustic but romantic cottage tucked into one of the many canyons that run through L.A. There were deer in the garden in the early mornings, yet we were only ten minutes from Beverly Hills. I had gone to get Gilles a Valentine's card and a box of chocolates and when I made the drive back up the winding canyon toward the cottage, I saw giant red banners strung high across the road at at least a dozen intervals, and each one was painted in white with funny and touching messages. I could never have imagined they were for me until I turned into the driveway and saw there was one more, but this one had both our names emblazoned in a giant heart. *I bought him a heart-shaped box of candy. How did I get this guy?* For a moment I was worried my entire relationship was like that season on *Dallas*, when it turned out it was all a dream.

But then Gilles stepped out of the gate with a cat-swallowed-the-canary grin. I threw myself at him in a move intended to replicate a romantic movie-moment where the girl jumps into her man's arms and he twirls her and then they kiss. In reality, I flew at Gilles and knocked him and me into a bottlebrush tree. The red spiky brushes broke off and showered us in leaves, red filaments, and dirt. But it did affirm that our relationship was no dream.

After some time, a friend suggested it was time for me to spread my wings and get a high profile Hollywood agent and he recommended me to a well connected someone he knew. A dose of reality jackhammered me when I dipped into my closet looking for something professional but easy to wear for my first meeting with the big and powerful Hollywood agent. My closet looked like it belonged to a schizophrenic: thin clothes, fat clothes, and the I-must-have-been-on-drugs-when-I-bought-those clothes, given the entire section of skimpy, vividly-patterned, and sleeveless flotsam that could only have looked good on a twenty-something who was size "zippedy-do-dah." A wave of depression washed over me. I had no idea anymore what I looked like. I had been on every diet known to mankind; low carbs, high carbs, and no carbs. I had played the yo-yo game like a gambler with an ever-full bucket of chips, and had lost and gained weight so often that when I passed my reflection in a store window I had no idea who I was looking at. I had lost sight of me. When I would pass a woman of some physical girth, I asked friends, "Is that what I look like?" They shook their heads, sure that I was fishing for something, not that they had a clue what it was. If I was having a *really* bad day, I pushed my imagination envelope and convinced myself that I looked like that 600-pound woman on the eleven o'clock news who needed to be carried on a double garage door by eight sweaty firemen after they knocked down the wall to her bedroom where she had survived on Cheetos for the last twenty years. Let me be clear, I *hate* Cheetos.

I pulled on my go-to stretchy jersey layers and tossed on an expensive and fabulous scarf, a pair of great boots, applied some hot lipstick and pushed all my self-loathing onto the back burner. Big girls usually put their money into the best accessories, because they always fit.

There is no more thrilling drive than Sunset Boulevard, passing one fabled mansion after another, each one seemingly replicated from the owner's favorite vacation destination: English Tudors, Côte d'Azur chateaus, Tuscan villas, Mexican haciendas, all competing for the most *oohs* and *aahs*. I never get over the staggering amount of tropical vegetation that lines the road before hitting the Strip, with its gigantic hand-painted billboards and iconic neon signs fronting music clubs, seen by the world through decades of movies. I was high on my own amazement that I lived there.

I pulled up in front of a cold but imposing office tower, handed my car off to a valet, and headed up the stairs to my future. I was about to enter the lobby that was the first line of defense to a fiefdom of power-brokers-to-the-stars, when a tight-limbed woman in a plaid miniskirt, thigh-high boots, and cascading blonde hair moved past me. I knew it was someone famous. Maybe Darryl Hannah? She stopped to put on a pair of giant sunglasses. I was sure she overheard my gasp! The woman, maybe someone famous in another life a long, long time ago, was ancient, and yet not. Her face seemed to be made of borrowed parts: lips that once belonged to a puffer fish, giant almond-shaped eyes that wouldn't close—the kind we had seen on renderings of imagined aliens. Her skin was so shiny; it was like a helium party balloon. I had seen so many of these new faces layered on those old faces; I had come to believe Los Angeles was the birthplace of a whole new tribe—never really younger, just bizarrely different. I hurried toward the security desk and signed in. I didn't want to have that image seared into my brain for another second.

I pressed the button for the elevator and was about to step in, when a trio of big-haired, overly protective she-beasts all dressed in black, pushed me aside so a very skinny giraffe carrying a giant purple purse could enter. *I had already seen enough weird to make that image seem real.* The three Meanies who were clearly there to protect the giraffe-like woman from any harm looked me over with disdain; my breasts were bigger than their heads. The giraffe backed up as if to get away from them. I stepped into the elevator and shrank into a corner, but with a quick glance, I saw it wasn't a giraffe. It was Margaux Hemingway. I waited for the coven and their charge to settle and I pressed the button to my floor. We rode up in interminable silence. Thank God. My floor. I stepped out and smacked straight into a teeny, perfect Drew Barrymore. She was the size of a teacup. I hurried down the hallway filled with framed photograph after photograph of famous faces: all frozen foreheads, strange lips, and blindingly white teeth.

I pushed open the gold-lettered door to an intentionally imposing office and was greeted by a scrawny frosted-haired, fierce-eyed banshee of a woman wearing a cashmere bandage dress thingy. She held out what might have been her hand but looked far more like a claw to me, and then she retracted it as she gave me the once-over. I knew instantly I was doomed. Disappointed that she had wasted her time, she cut to the chase, and in a hardened, fast-talking New Jersey accent she said she would not be representing me, despite being sure I was a very talented person. Then, lasering me with her cold fish eyes, she added, "This is million dollar pearls so listen very carefully. You should go back to wherever it is that you came from; lose forty, fifty, maybe even sixty pounds. Bleach those teeth, lighten and brighten your hair. And let me wrap up by saying again, go home, lose the weight. This is no place, no matter how talented and I'm sure you are, for 'big' girls."

I smiled and thanked her for her time and such valuable advice, but when I got to the door, I turned and said, "I hope to prove you wrong." I wish I'd had the presence of mind to say, "What difference does my size make? I'm a writer!"

As I hurried away toward the elevator, I saw a stairwell. The sign said, "Roof." For a very brief moment I thought about going up there and throwing myself off. This was Hollywood and ooh, big surprise, I had once again broken the law against fat people. There was probably a special task force that wrote tickets and stuck them on our asses.

I arrived home spent and shriveled like an old balloon. The witchy-agent had made it abundantly clear that I wasn't welcome in Tinsel-Town. Whatever confidence I had built up from having the best, most amazing husband and some success as a writer and actress, was now shattered. I took all my pain out on Gilles. I was a short, fat troll and he was my pusher. The man was skinny but he kept bringing me croissants and apricot jam-filled baguettes. I knew I should say no. *Do I look like someone who knows how to do that?* He cooked all the time, and not a slab of chicken followed by boiled string beans; instead he made golden brown, butter-infused chicken with an au gratin, orgasm-inducing potato side dish. If its scent was wafting under my nose, of course I was going to eat it. I was weak. My will power only existed when our fridge was empty. "Stop cooking!" He looked at me as if I had slapped him. I tried to explain that I couldn't continue to be held hostage by food. He said he wouldn't cook for me anymore. Neither of us was happy. But I was determined to beat the odds even if I had to nail my mouth shut. I could see Gilles was worried about me but he knew when I was in this kind of place, it was best to keep *his* mouth shut. If only I could do the same.

Back on the hunt for something, anything that would help me lose weight. I asked around and I found a guy who sold some magic pills guaranteed to have you dropping fifty pounds in fifty minutes. I went to his place in a none-too savory part of town and handed him a check for $120. He handed me a dozen small baggies filled with little green pellets. I opened one of them as I got into the car. The pellets smelled disgusting and a lot like fish food. I sighed and tossed them into an open garbage can before I inserted the key in the ignition. *Once again, money well spent.*

But I kept going. I took meeting after meeting with prospective agents. *When a door closes and there ain't no windows, rip up a floorboard. Don't quit.* I didn't, and eventually I landed a believer—a wonderful caring agent and I got jobs, lots of jobs. I was happy to be the sidekick, the best friend, the madam, the therapist. I got writing jobs: good ones and bad ones, but I was building a resume. And again, I did what I did best. I made friends and the more I really got to know them, the more I understood that everyone had demons, challenges, good days and bad. Being there for each other was the one thing we could do, until we were able to get ourselves on track, or not. Those friends, along with Gilles, were my ticket. They became my mentors, my connections, and part of my circle of salvation.

One of those friends, Bill, thought the best way to keep me aloft was by pulling outrageous pranks on me, requiring me to keep my wits and my humor about me. On a flight back to Los Angeles from Toronto, a flight attendant came over the intercom, asking Monica Parker to identify herself. I thought they must have me confused with someone who preordered a special meal but I waved anyway. A very authoritative steward approached and in a loud whisper assured me that my doctor had contacted the airlines and, given that I was to have surgery the next day, I was to have nothing by mouth other than water. Again, I thought they must have mixed me up with another passenger. He double-checked his paper and insisted it was, in fact, me. In that moment, I knew who the prankster was and I tried, to no avail, to explain, but Mr. Busybody wasn't having any of it. He implied my "doctor" suggested I might say that. Needless to say, I was ravenous and a bit cranky when I got off that five-hour plane ride.

After several smaller attacks, Bill got me again. It was my birthday and Gilles happened to be away. Bill called and said he had a surprise for me. I felt a chill travel up my spine. What did he have in store for me this time? It must be said that Bill was smart, incredibly entertaining, and always there for me when I really needed him. I took a deep breath and said okay. Three hours later, we were still driving. We were far, far away from Beverly Hills and most definitely not in Kansas. We were deep into the sprawl of the San Fernando Valley where most of the buildings were industrial and low to the ground. Auto body repair shops, defunct photo labs, and a couple of Mexican taco stands stood between large swaths of shuttered manufacturing plants that had begun to disintegrate under the relentless canopies of trumpet vines, all set against the haze of the Verdugo Mountains. The more I grilled him, the more Bill would smile and say, "Oh just go with it . . ." We pulled up to a small, squat, red brick building in the middle of Nothingville. Dusk was falling and Bill got out and rang the buzzer of a barred doorway. My radar was sounding off alarms. The porthole in the door opened, and I heard Bill say, "She's here." As a writer, I am relentlessly curious and usually up for almost any window into other worlds but my gut was telling me I was not going to be looking through a window on this adventure. Bill pretty much had to drag me out of the car. The door flung open and I was confronted by a pair of what appeared to be dominatrices.

I was introduced to Mistress Carmen and Mistress Bella. They were both wearing black corsets, fishnets, and very high heels, along with their own signature accessories: studded dog collars, matching handcuffs, and what looked like chain-link fence accoutrements. Of course they both had the obligatory plummy-black lipstick and matching nails. In that moment, I really wanted to be home with a large bowl of comforting noodle-anything and a book . . . a wholesome one. But when my surprise mistress-duo began singing "Happy Birthday" to me in high squeaky voices, I burst out laughing and thought Bill to be the funniest man on the planet. If only that had been the end of it.

At the end of the "hip, hip, hoorays," Mistress Carmen took my hand and brought me inside. I turned to grab Bill, but he was already heading toward his car. He smiled, winked, and said, "Just go with it" and he was gone. I stood in the foyer, a fancy word for the hallway into a sad little derelict room with bad wood paneling and a stringy-haired man drinking a beer, eyes glued to a small TV in the corner. Mistress Carmen led me, as if I was going to my own death, into an even smaller room with a massage table strung with manacles, leather straps, and switches. An assortment of high spiky heels, whips, and chains were within arm's reach. *Not my arms!* By this time, I had broken into a cold sweat as I stood frozen, feeling much like a child must when entering a spooky Halloween haunted house. My mouth hung slack-jawed, my eyes were as big as saucers, and I had no saliva left to swallow with. Mistress Carmen asked if I'd like a Pepsi. "Yes, please."

She left the room and, as I let out my breath, I began planning my escape—and Bill's murder. Too late, she was back carrying two frosty cans of soda. She handed one to me and said, "Bondage or discipline?"

I do believe I felt that most Victorian of maladies; I became weak in the knees. "I don't know." *I didn't want to know. Oh God, my very own* Fifty Shades of Grey! (Oh wait, that wasn't written yet. But you get my drift.) The sugar from the soda hit its mark, and although I knew the rush would be short, my wits had returned and I asked, "Have you been paid for this time with me?" She said yes. I continued, "Then you don't care what we do with our time?"

She shook her long reedy hair and my Mistress very clearly said, "It's your money, but I don't do girls." *Good to know.* It was then that I told her I was a writer and would she be okay if we just spent the time talking. I had a lot to learn. The pair of us girls sat on the massage table, swinging our legs, and chatted like old friends. I found out Carmen, real name Cleo, had been a prostitute on the mean streets of Hollywood and had been severely beaten a couple of times, but as in many fun fairy tales, she had married her pimp and now only worked inside and "did nuthin' sexual." She told me that on Sundays, the place was packed with "sinners" wanting to have their punishment for whatever bad deeds they had committed that week meted out by whichever doms were on duty. Cleo laughed and said that "The Church of Discipline" had been registered as a house of worship, and therefore was tax exempt.

My hour was almost up when Cleo asked me if I wanted to scare my friend who had dropped me off there by having a couple of rope marks on my wrists. It was my turn to laugh. "Good idea!" Bill was sitting outside, an odd look on his face, when Cleo and I hugged each other and I walked to the car rubbing my wrists. I refused to explain.

It wasn't long before I got my revenge, with Gilles' help. About a month later, he called Bill, asking him if he would mind picking me up at my doctor's office because he was busy with a client. When Bill arrived, one of the nurses asked him to wait in another room. My doctor, a friend and a great sport, sat down in front of him and said he would be happy to discuss his imminent vasectomy in detail. He said, "Your sister Monica explained how very shy you are, Bill. I'd like to allay your fears. It's a very quick snip and the blood leakage is minimal." My doctor pal offered some very graphic statistics as Bill paled and babbled that he was not my brother, backing out of the room. It did little to curtail Bill's endless enthusiasm for practical jokes, but I did enjoy his next birthday gift, a portrait of me done on black velvet, replete with a flashing diamond tooth.

Gilles was unable to stay out of the kitchen and within a couple of weeks I could no longer resist the aromas permeating the entire house. *Bastard.* We ate and drank wine and I thought there had to be a better way to deal with my body issues. I decided to take up exercise, but unless dragged by a team of runaway horses, there was no way I was going to a gym in Beverly Hills. I had ventured into a couple of them when we first arrived. They were all filled to capacity with highly motivated young actresses, singers, weather girls, and tight-assed blondes, sipping their daily caloric intake from water bottles. I felt like I had stumbled into an all-female army that marched absolutely in unison to the same drummer. When I caught my reflection in the mirror, my arms going in the wrong direction and my bent-over ass eclipsing at least two of the now-irate skinny things who couldn't see around me, I knew being there was a worse idea than choosing to sit at the epicenter of the San Andreas Fault, knowing an earthquake was imminent.

Of course, Gilles found the perfect solution. I worked out, not in a public gym but in my garage. There were two spaces, but we only had one car and we weren't that worried about it getting scratched. He partitioned it off and lined one wall with mirrors including a pull curtain in case I was in a self-loathing state of mind. First I tried a "dreadmill," but it didn't take long for me to feel like a large, imprisoned hamster on its perpetually moving belt. I sent it back and bought a stationary recumbent bicycle, so sure this was to be my machine of choice. It hurt my knees and felt so unsatisfying to have pedaled for so long to end up going nowhere. Luckily I bought it on sale so felt little remorse when it soon enough embraced its new life as a clothes rack. I tried jogging but my boobs kept hitting me in my ears. *Maybe speed walking encased in head-to-toe Lycra? What was wrong with looking like a jiggling, turquoise and hot-pink bratwurst windup toy?* I bought a giant yellow plastic bouncy ball. It reminded me of being a kid, until I tried some real fat-burning moves on it and landed repeatedly on my ass. I left it on the curb where it was soon picked up by some other wanna-be.

Everyone in Beverly Hills had a personal trainer. I knew it would be expensive but maybe that would turn the tide. I put out the word and was flooded with recommendations. I chose a German woman who sounded kindly and confident that together we would break the cycle of failure that she felt was mostly mental. Her name was Gudren and I hired her sight unseen. I was excited—a trainer who was part shrink—I would be getting a two-fer. In the same way some of us clean their houses before their cleaning ladies come, I thought I'd better get in shape before my trainer met me. I strapped on my double-cushioned, hundred-dollar running shoes and ventured out into the smog and dry-as-flour air to hit the pavement. Twenty minutes later, I was winded and my knees were in danger of buckling. I crawled back home and lay on the couch, with a small bag of potato chips to replenish my energy.

I was so excited to begin my guru-lead exercise routine that I made cookies to welcome Gudren into my life. A fully tattooed and muscular she-bitch from hell stomped through our front door and took over. First she led me to my kitchen and hovered over me like a vigilant maximum-security guard, just to make sure I dumped the cookies into the garbage can. The soft-spoken phone voice was a sham, a come-on to lure people with her warm, lulling demeanor. I had been suckered.

One week later, the beat of some hard-pumping disco dance-to-the-death music was blasting from a set of speakers set on the hood of our car in *my gym*. My new Nazi-trainer's voice cut through it all, screaming, "Hit the deck and give me fifty! And stop staring!" The woman was a human billboard but didn't want to be looked at. She didn't seem to notice or care that I was far from being in Navy Seal shape as she bludgeoned me into yet another murderous round of deep, butt-burning crunches. This woman had not one iota of compassion or sensitivity; she pushed and pushed and all I could feel was my burning resistance to being pushed. I was exhausted, parched, and getting more upset by the moment. I had fifty that I wanted to give her but it wasn't push-ups, more like stab wounds to her every artery. I didn't respond well to being yelled at. But I was more afraid of quitting than I was of having a heart attack. I couldn't handle failure, seeing as I had invited the bitch into my life. I bit down and pushed myself harder, visualizing my long lean body piercing through the layers of fat, continuing on until it pierced her, right through to the place where her heart was supposed to be, until she was seriously dead on my garage floor.

21

Wine Making

Diet #24 ✦ **All the Fruit One Can Eat**

Cost ✦ **Minimal–It was California**

Weight lost ✦ **12 liters of bodily fluids**

Weight gained ✦ **13 liters of bodily fluids**

I woke up at three in the morning, tossing and turning, dripping in flop sweat after three weeks of nonstop abuse. I was agonizing about how to dump the trainer from hell and it was causing me sleepless nights. Even the word "trainer" conjured up nightmarish images of a sadistic ringmaster wearing black leather riding boots and carrying a sharp-cracking riding crop, standing over me, a cowering fat woman covered in bandages. I wanted her gone. I couldn't unload her in person, as it might prove to be dangerous; she could break me in half. A letter would take too long. Hiring a hit man would come back to bite me, but that was my favorite scenario. He could make her eat her damn Kettle ball. I sat up in bed in agony from the searing workout pains running through every part of my body. I felt Gilles rubbing my back. "What's wrong? Why are you awake?" I told him I had to fire Frau Trainer, but I didn't know how. As always he had an easy, commonsense solution: "Tell her you are done and you won't be needing her services anymore." He yawned and went back to sleep. He clearly didn't know Ms. Barbell-Breath; she believed in the art of war. She ate children for breakfast. These were the days before texting and e-mails allowed us to chicken out of anything in a faceless and cowardly way.

It was barely seven in the morning but I was armed with a glazed doughnut and a cup of very strong black coffee as I dialed, praying for the strength to spit it out and then hang up. Her answering machine picked up. *Oh thank God.* But then I heard that soft, sweet lying voice and I shivered. I spat it out all right, "You're fired!" I hung up, realizing I didn't even say who was calling—but she'd know my whipped and whiny voice anywhere. I was about to take a huge bite of my doughnut, when I remembered: I had just spent weeks working my tail off. How much weight had the bitch screamed off me? I was excited. "I'll be a sylph—a string-bean size 14." I went to the bathroom to weigh myself, so sure that this time . . . Oh my God, I had gained muscle weight and I was still dragging around an ass big enough to double as a shelf. I measured myself. Instead of being a size 22, I was now a size 20! Big whoop-de-do! I needed something radical and I didn't care if it was rat poison. I took a huge bite of the doughnut. I had to get this damn weight off. But first, I needed to take a three-day nap.

* * *

An anorexic, second-tier, thrice married but now very much single, former movie-star neighbor, who always carried a packet of dog-eared, yellowed photographs and clippings of her glory days in her ancient Hermes Birkin handbag, had befriended me. Cassandra was lonely and alone, and seemed to always have one eye on her window to see the comings and goings of the neighborhood. Whenever she saw me coming in and out of my garden gate, she somehow managed to whip out of her house and block my path. She was deeply interested in the ongoing saga of my losing battle with the bulge. She fancied herself something of a New Age practitioner of all things natural. She carried oversized pillboxes filled with herbal everything from sleep aids to stool softeners. She didn't understand when I told her she reminded me of my father. She had jumbo bottles filled with fish oil, bee pollen, magnesium, ginkgo-biloba, and it was all stuffed into that bag along with the clippings and a pair of ben-wa balls. *You are on your own for that one.* I had barely set foot on the sidewalk when Cassandra blocked my path and excitedly invited me over for tea at her place. She had been talking to a friend who was visiting, when she saw me and thought I would find Roselby very interesting. "She's a High Priestess."

"Of what?" I asked.

Cassandra said, "Of living food."

From a girl who was willing to eat rat poison just a few hours ago, I didn't feel I had the right to judge anyone. I sat down with Cassandra, right under an enormous full-length portrait of herself looking as she wished she still did when she was under contract to a film studio 110 years ago. Roselby, sitting across from us, was the picture of health, if gaunt was your thing, and I so wanted it to be mine. I hung on every word as she messianically assured me that a six-week regime of nothing but fruit would change my metabolic set point forever. I had no idea what that meant but it was just fruit, nothing weird. Cassandra promised me Roselby was the best. Everyone went to her. I was in. I loved fruit.

I committed to the All-You-Can-Eat-Fruit-Diet, which came with the guarantee that I could eat all day and yet still lose acreage. It consisted of bushels of berries, casaba melons by the truckload, papayas, mangoes, whole vineyards of grapes, pineapple, and dozens of pears. At first I was ecstatic; there was no counting and no weighing. I ate as if I were a happy baboon, picking fruit right off the trees, although I did have to spend an inordinate amount of time visiting the deluxe bathrooms of Beverly Hills. But then, like most too-much-of-a-good thing, it began to get old, and my mind began to drift into dreams of German chocolate cake. I couldn't look at another guava.

Gilles stepped in to the rescue. He began serving me all my meals. My breakfasts were bowls of berries pretending to be cereal with an accompanying milk pitcher filled with water. Lunches came disguised as two huge slabs of watermelon filled with mashed mango, as if it were a sandwich. Dinners were amazing: plates heaped with papaya-slices cut to look like a mountain of french fries, watermelon steaks, and pear puree in a sundae cup for dessert. Three weeks later, horrible painful cramps began to set in. I could barely stand up. Gilles immediately brought me a piece of toast with peanut butter but I refused to eat it. I wanted this to work. Within two days, I was sitting cramped over in my doctor's office, swearing I would never buy into anyone's assertion, no matter how well intentioned, that they knew the best tinker, tailor, doctor, vet, or hair-colorist and absolutely the "best diet ever." *Bull* . . . After a fairly quick analysis of my fling with nothing but fruit, the doctor gave me his diagnosis. I was fermenting. *I was making wine in my kidneys!* I would have laughed had the cramping not kicked in again.

I was a mess and now terrified of food, believing every mouthful arrived loaded with calories and anxiety; my mouth was a portal to hell. I knew how to go into the food monastery and take a vow of starvation, it was when I stepped into the land of the eaters I was doomed. I had no understanding of middle ground. I knew how to be a pig at the trough or a twig-eating nut ball. There were millions and millions of pounds lost each year along with millions and millions of dollars. I decided to get off the diet train and try something completely foreign, a balanced lifestyle.

This resolution lasted about a minute in my diet time line; in reality, it was probably about two weeks in, when my upstairs neighbor, Linda, who was no stranger to the art of celebration—in fact I would have to anoint her The Queen—invited me to a party. Every February 14th, Linda had an all girls' Valentine's Day luncheon that started at noon and ended when the last chocolate heart had melted.

Linda was a woman who loved hearts and she pulled out all the stops on this annual rite of passage. Hearts were everywhere, made of crystal, flowers, straw, paper, porcelain, and, even better, cheese and chocolate. The lunch plates were heart-shaped as was every hanging bauble and there was a plethora. It was a *tour de force* of excess. We were instructed to wear only red, pink, purple, or white, and at every turn there was a photo op, where we all looked like bunches of pretty peonies. (One year I wore green and almost lost my place.) But it was the platters of delicious heart-shaped sandwiches, quiches, tarts, and pies that did me in. Much like a panda deprived of bamboo, I ate the entire forest.

Year in year out, regardless of which diet I was on and I'm sure I was on one every year, my willpower would rarely accompany me through the front door on those heart days. This lunch was a hot and much-desired ticket; there was only room for a dozen women and all of us treasured our special seats at the most fun table in town. It started with everyone bringing a gift for Linda, but then one year, one of the girls brought a gift for each guest, and so it began. From then on we all went home lugging eleven over-the-top but never-ever expensive presents, wrapped and primped like no other. It had become quite competitive in its inventiveness and who doesn't love wholesale Swarovski crystal eyeglasses, tiaras, cowboy hats, boas, bracelets, and on and on. In spite of the gathering being a collection of well-known actresses, power brokers, and independent thinkers, this was the most unabashed girl-fiesta anywhere, and a true testament to how much laughter and love women have for each other. But what did we talk about while drinking pink martini's and noshing on sumptuous heart-shaped berry and cream scones, besides our love lives? It was all about the latest diets that most of us would be on soon enough, regardless of what shape our bodies were in. There was something sad about that.

As Julia Child said, "A party without cake is just a meeting."

I still had my personal gym but I no longer had Gudren, the she-wolf, so I had no fear about pushing the button on our garage opener and going inside. There stood the recumbent bike under a pile of coats, and sticking out of bins were the bits and pieces of exercise paraphernalia I had bought and then sold and probably bought back again at various garage sales: two mini trampolines, a ThighMaster, walking weights, dumbbells, an Ab Blaster, ropes, pulleys, a broken rowing machine, and various forms of transportation from bicycles to Rollerblades. The whole collection appeared to have eyes, all looking at me in condemnation. I threw a coat over the bins so I couldn't see their scorn and picked up a jump rope, contemplating stringing them all up, but then I took it into the backyard and began clumsily to skip rope. For a short while I felt like a happy four-year-old, but the beating my chin was taking from being hit by those damn boobs, along with a sudden seizing in my left hip, put an end to that activity. I dropped the rope and left the garden on foot. It started with an exploration of my neighborhood, one step at a time, and before I knew it, an hour had passed. So began my lifelong joy of walking. No equipment required. I parked all of the fitness crap outside on the sidewalk and posted a sign that said, "Free."

My evening walks were magical. The perfume from the night-blooming jasmine, lime and orange trees, and rose gardens wafted

around me. The air was always cool and the softly lit glow from
the houses gave any décor-voyeur an aspirational window into the
beautiful homes en route to the business triangle and Rodeo Drive
with all its platinum brands: Neiman Marcus, Barneys, Saks, Chanel,
Louis Vuitton. They were all places that had nothing to do with
my life but it was fun to pretend, except, even in fantasy, the clothes
were too tight.

Unfortunately, the triangle was also home to some of my favorite restaurants; The Cheescake Factory being at the top of my list,
filled with infinite mouthwatering varieties of dessert luring me in.
Reese's peanut butter chocolate cake cheesecake, banana cream pie
cheesecake, and dulce de leche caramel cheesecake were just the tip
of the sugar tree. They had the power of Sirens, calling out in their
come-hither voices to those of us whose willpower was always on a
sliding scale, to follow them to wherever danger lay. I could never
resist. Just like in "Cheers," all the waiters knew my name.

I was not alone. Food has become a national neurosis. Instead of
bringing sustenance and pleasure, we're warned that this road can
only lead to unhappiness. We've been made to feel as if we have
committed a capital crime simply because we like dessert. When
I look at the black-and-white photographs of our ancestors, who
came in all shapes and sizes, they seem a lot less obsessed and anxious than we've become. Possibly, because they had a lot less time
on their hands to worry about what they ate, just that they needed
to. *Oh, that old Devil's playground.*

22

Body of Evidence

Diet #25 ✦ **Hypnosis**

Cost ✦ **$600.00**

Weight lost ✦ **Some**

Weight gained ✦ **Some more**

T here was so much to celebrate in our California life, not the least of which was the gorgeous weather, but it was a lesson to be careful what you wish for. The relentless sun, which I was no fan of with my white British skin, came with the need to wear sleeveless things, which was anathema to my unofficial Canadian Bill of Rights, specifically: *the right not to bare arms.* No matter how hot it got I never succumbed to wearing shorts either, preferring to hide myself under thin layers of gauzy material. Gilles and I moved into a gorgeous Spanish duplex with an enormous banana palm tree right outside our bedroom window. It filled me with joy every morning when I woke up. Everything about that tree was sexy: its fronds undulating in warm winds with clusters of bananas ripe for the picking, reminding me how lucky we were to be exactly where we were. We ate breakfast outside almost every day under the shade of a beautiful willow tree that sparkled at night with a hundred twinkle lights.

Our new home became a mecca for a never-ending parade of smart, funny people, many of whom, like us, had come to L.A. to join the ranks of nomadic actors and writers all seeking their place in the sun. They often joined us at our courtyard dinner table where Gilles served up meals and we all served up fun. But my secret self was feeling like a failure. Mostly I was embarrassed; why could I not lose this weight? *"Well," said my doctor who was also a friend, "it seems you like to face your danger zones head on, by sitting endlessly at a table laden with food. You could try bowling instead."*

My problem became magnified in this town, which attracted the most beautiful people in the world, and I was only too willing to use that as an excuse. But I knew I had brought this neurosis with me all the way from Scotland, via Canada; it wasn't born in L.A. The part I really struggled with had less to do with my weight and more to do with why I cared so much about my weight. Intellectually I had this covered, but emotionally, not so much. Was it my constant shape-shifting that made me have so little sense of self? One would think I would be used to that. It was all I'd ever known. Sometimes, I thought it was because I had grown tired of the tap dance; I had been working to get noticed and be loved since I was a little girl. Yes, I had baggage, who didn't? But I still felt these were superficial ideas. Why couldn't I have been more like some of my heroes? Jane Goodall, a renowned primatologist and pacifist, devoted her life to caring for the protection of chimpanzees in the wilds of Tanzania. She probably didn't give a damn about how she was perceived physically. Of course she only hung out with hairy big-bottomed chimpanzees, who had a very different set of priorities for what they wanted from a woman. Bananas! And Gloria Steinem, a brilliant journalist, eschewed all makeup and artifice to get her message of feminism across to a generation; of course the fact that she had already been a Playboy Bunny most likely gave her confidence to do without lipstick and a bra.

The complicated part for me was that it took me so long to believe I was attractive. I had grown up with far too many mixed messages on that front, although I'm pretty sure that could be said for most people. If we were to go back and look at the photos of our twenty-two-year-old selves, we'd see we were beautiful. We just didn't have the confidence to know it and that is the irony. Being attractive is so much more than just being pretty; it is about the whole package, replete with energy, kindness, humor, brains, a forgiving heart and, for me, one of the biggies—authenticity. But having knowledge doesn't always mean we are capable of applying it. That sometimes requires a lifetime of trial and error. I was very good at both. Hopefully I would be given a long life. It appeared I would need it.

I really shouldn't have worried about being superficial, given I was living in the land that bred the highest achievers in that category. I was surrounded by movie stars and models, all armed with black belts in the art of show-not-tell.

One morning Gilles and I were at our neighborhood grocery store when I overheard him talking to a very attractive, curvy, older woman who was knocking back some giant green drink. He commented on the concoction and she, in a very frustrated voice, responded that she had been drinking these spinach-kale-apple things for months and hadn't dropped an ounce. He looked at her and, as only Gilles could get away with, suggested that perhaps she was intended to be beautiful and curvy. She practically cried at the compliment but then looked at him and said; "You're not from around here are you?"

It truly was a whole other world. One of my neighbors, a stunning woman who was probably in her mid forties but looked only thirty-something, as is the law of this land, confided in me that she was leaving her boring, lawyer husband. She hadn't broken the news to him yet, as she needed to get all that she could from him and then shore it up before he found out and went ballistic with the full force of his law firm behind him. Having been privy to what happens to many former wives of successful men, she went in for breast augmentation surgery, teeth bleaching, and hair extensions. Her unwitting, soon-to-be-ex thought she was doing this as a gift for him and he more than happily nursed her back to health.

When she was healed, she took to showing almost everyone her new and improved curb appeal, even if they weren't interested in being given a viewing. I was provided the privilege over breakfast. *Eggs sunny side-up were served, how perfect.* One early morning after her car pool, she stopped by to flash me. What does one say . . . "Nice work"? I got it. She was leaving her man and would be hunting new game imminently; therefore redoing her breasts was akin to arming the warheads in preparation. By the time her tough-guy lawyer hubby was served notice, she was already hooked up with even bigger game and had the big fat diamond ring ready to pop on her finger to prove it. It was just another story in the almost naked city, but there were so many and they surrounded me.

Another beauty, Liza, who had recently moved in upstairs with two other beauties from the Barbie-doll catalogue, was truly stunning, warm, friendly—and very insecure. Once again, I couldn't put an age on her and that was exactly the effect she wanted. She had been on the dating scene for far too long and was finally with a man who was ready to close the deal and marry her. He was handsome in a stuffed-shirt way and appeared to be harmless but for some reason, instead of being happy, Liza was jittery and tense. It was the end of the day and we were sitting outside on the steps when I asked her what was wrong. She explained she was a nervous wreck and didn't want to blow it but she was terrified to live with him because then he would find out how much money it actually cost to be *her*. Her monthly maintenance cost more than his Beverly Hills condo fees. Yikes! It was hard to imagine what Liza was having done every month that could rack up those bills so, of course, I asked. Other than the expected—teeth whitening, hair extensions, *natural* highlighting, and full waxing—there was something called Thermage, which tightened the skin with some high-tech, roller-like apparatus; bimonthly vampire face-lifts, *not kidding*, fillers using one's own blood; and, my favorite, migraine management, which I was in need of just at the thought of being that high maintenance. If I were to seek that level of perfection, they would have to throw a drop cloth over me and shut me down like they did the Statue of Liberty for at least a year. There would be scaffolding and men at work—masons, a variety of sandblasters, artisans skilled in the art of sculpting, and then a team of painters and paper-hangers. And at the end of it all, I still wouldn't be able to wear a thong. In that moment, I was so glad to be me. It cost mere pennies to have me be this undone. Liza and so many women like her put themselves through so much to get approval, not knowing they were already beautiful. It was tragic that they felt they weren't enough just as they were. But it was just as tragic that I couldn't get that message myself. "*Ding. Ding. Epiphany alert . . . oooooo.*

You would think at this point I might have found a therapist . . . but I had British-European roots. We didn't go to therapy; we nailed one foot to the floor and spun faster, believing that would solve our problems.

There was no making sense of the business I was in. Success could come as a result of talent, hard work, or a lucky break, but only if blessed by fate, connections, and a dollop of magic. There was no rhyme or reason for any of it. To be an actor, one had to have faith and another career. Show business was random, as if written on a Magic Slate, with far too much downtime. I was dangerously bored and I could feel myself sliding backward into childhood habits: eating too fast, too much and then hiding the evidence, candy wrappers instantly shoved to the bottom of trash baskets. If I didn't see them, the crime had not happened. There were secret trips to the market to stuff my face with potato chips and peanut-butter cups before I was even out of the store; chocolates that didn't stand a chance of surviving the night were tucked into recesses of cabinets and drawers. I blamed my slide on all manner of failures, which was really the flip side of fear. Excuses, I had a million of them: too much unemployment—mostly mine; overfishing—I didn't want to miss out on real crab salad; our dependence on oil—good Italian olive oil was so expensive.

I was angry that I continually hobbled myself, and Gilles tried to make me feel better by telling me he loved my appetite. By the look on my face, he immediately knew I had taken that the wrong way. He spoke quickly, "It is your appetite for living the big life, not about eating but for having fun, for being interested in everything that brings so much to me, to my life." And for an accidental but not so sweet icing, he added; "You make jokes, but I think they are real. Maybe not so many jokes would be better." All his assurances were interpreted by my inner-Gestapo as packs of lies! What the hell was his deal? What jokes? Didn't he see the planet was overpopulated and we were in danger of running out of food? That would be very bad for him, given how irritable I would become.

I didn't want to feel bad; I was not good at it. I sunk lower and lower, wishing he would leave me so I could close the blinds and put on the old flannel nightie, not an item of clothing I would ever have worn in my marital bed. *I had sexy onesies with feet and a trap door for that.* I wanted to take to my bed with several large tubs of ice cream and not have any witnesses. He had struck a nerve. He wanted to fix me and that made things worse. I was not a vacuum cleaner; well I was, but not in the way he meant. I was not an appliance that could have its dials adjusted. *If only.*

As usual, a bolt of clarity arrived just before dawn when everything was dangerously quiet. I understood what Gilles was saying to me. I was stuck playing an old tape in my head, one that screamed at me that I wasn't good enough, so I made jokes in order to deflect and erase the negative. Funny thing, people were always trying to protect me from myself whenever I would make a smart-ass or disparaging joke about my body, but I didn't need that kind of protection. The jokes were not the problem. I liked jokes; they gave me perspective and they allowed me to throw up a smoke screen while examining the work in progress that was me. They let me spit everything out in ways that made me laugh and kept anyone else from tearing me down. These jokes were not self-sabotage, just the opposite in fact; I felt quite detached from them. Sometimes, funny is just funny. But what was true was how I behaved, not what I said.

Something shifted and it wasn't comfortable. I needed to change that tape; I needed to find a better way to handle stress. The habit of stuffing my face when my demons reared their ugly heads was the real problem. These demons, the ones we all have, are bigger than we are. They *are* demons! They had fire and serpent-like tails that could crush all my good intentions. The idea that I could control them suddenly seemed ridiculous. I was loved deeply, by Gilles and by so many other people. Not once did he judge me. It was time for me to change the tape, get over myself, and find a better way.

I hauled myself out of bed, cleaned myself up, and found a hypno-therapist. The practice had been around for six thousand years; I figured if they could make legions of people quack like ducks and flap their arms like chickens, they might be able to get me to shut my mouth.

Dr. Victor was a very nice man with a very good reputation but he had his work cut out for him when he met me. He was quite clear when he said it would most likely take several sessions to see a change, as shifting an ingrained belief system didn't happen with the snap of some fingers the way it was shown on television. He explained that I would retain total control, even when he put me under, and assured me I wouldn't do anything I didn't want to do. It was more like a truly deep state of relaxation, all the clatter stilled, allowing for hypnotic suggestion to have a place to land. With the rules explained, I was ready to play the game. I was a little disappointed Dr. Victor didn't use a dangling pocket watch swinging back and forth to lull me into a deep trance. He simply spoke in a calm and steady way much like in a yoga meditation, and the more he spoke and guided me through some deep breathing, the more I felt the chatterboxes slowing down. They were still there waiting to get back in control but somehow I didn't want them to. It was when he began talking about my body, guiding me through visualizations that were supposed to change the way I saw myself, that I could feel the chatterboxes stir to life. They resented being managed and they resisted. And the more he talked, the more I felt he was talking about someone else. That smaller-waisted woman he wanted me to see and believe in was not me. Putting my head on that body was not a good fit. I felt the chatterboxes rise up in unison, and we were done. Bye-bye *hippotherapy*.

The experience reminded me of a dinner-party story a psychotherapist friend of mine had told me. I was pretty sure it was apocryphal but it was still a good tale. A woman had been referred to a therapist because she had begun walking down a staircase as if she were carrying something heavy. She did the same thing when she sat and she always twisted her body to allow for whatever she was carrying when she passed through a door frame. After several sessions she revealed she was carrying a treasure chest in her head and it kept her awake at night because she couldn't ever get comfortable. After a few months of talk therapy that wasn't getting anywhere and several consultations with a psychiatrist colleague, they got the woman's permission to perform surgery to remove it. The doctors all knew it was psychosomatic but very real to her. She was admitted to the hospital and she was put under, her head shaved and bandaged. When she woke up, they told her the surgery had been successful and they had removed the treasure chest. Lying next to her on the bedside table they had placed a large chest filled with baubles and coins. She took one look at it and said. "That's not mine." I knew exactly what she meant.

Sitting outside that evening, I told Gilles that, while feeling deeply relaxed, I still had a touch of a night watchman's vigilance when being asked to accept Dr. Victor's very positive imagery, which I felt was similar to wanting me to believe I was driving a fully kitted-out Ferrari after having spent years in a very comfy four-door sedan.

I sat outside for a long time, thinking about the hundreds of pounds I had dropped over my life and how often they were called back for active duty. And still, with all my introspection and self-awareness, I didn't believe I was intended to be fat. Something *had* gone wrong in the shipping department; they had sent out my head attached to the wrong body.

23

Butter

Cost ✦ **$1,500 but not for food**

Weight lost ✦ **None**

Weight gained ✦ **Sure**

I wanted a baby. I didn't *really* want a baby. I wanted to stop thinking about my body. I wanted to be *legally* fat. Gilles was apprehensive and it surprised me to witness my man being fearful of anything. He was the one always rushing to my side to bear the brunt of whatever obstacle, emotional or physical, that might be panicking me. He couldn't or wouldn't put into words what was bothering him, so I tried playing twenty questions to see if could get him to explain what was freaking him out. He just kept saying he wasn't ready. It didn't make sense; this man was the most ready person I knew.

I tried wheedling, pleading, and then negotiating. "Honey, honey, come on, we have plants and they are doing well; well, surviving mostly. We're great doggie parents buying the best treats, and she's extremely popular with all the other dogs at the park, if not their owners."

It all became clear when Gilles said, "Dogs are not babies. Babies are expensive." It was about money. But then I began to think it was more about being responsible for someone's life, not just financially, but in every way and forever. It was a daunting prospect, the notion of becoming a parent, putting us right on the fast track to adulthood. And for Gilles, that required pause and reflection. It was about looking at all sides as if every question was like a tetrahedron. It was part of his process; he needed to look at all the pros and cons, and then decide. For me, it took the blink of an eye. I relished snap decisions; this was where I had absolute confidence in that I trusted my gut.

I tried to leave it alone and allow him the time he needed, but he needed a lot of time. Just sitting in a restaurant while he ordered from the menu was an exercise in the art of Zen. Not my forte. I was fidgeting and twitching like a four-year-old while he ruminated. I had had enough. I was on a mission and I didn't want to be given a no. *I didn't like no.* I leapt onto him and thrust my chest in his face. "Babies are cheap . . . look at these tatas and think of a neon-lit, full-service, open twenty-four-seven bar. What baby wouldn't want to sidle up to that watering hole? Children may be expensive, but by then we'll have lots and lots of money, won't we?" Gilles, good naturedly, said he certainly hoped so, because he knew I wouldn't let this go until he gave in. He thought the giving in part might be fun.

Wham! Bam! I was pregnant. Gilles was over the moon; it was me who turned out to be the nervous Nellie. What had we done? *I knew what we had done.* We had bought tickets on the biggest roller coaster and it had left the station and there was no way to get off. I couldn't sleep; what if I turned out to be just like my mother? She had all these really great qualities and she couldn't have loved me more, but she wasn't a great mother.

I was standing at the stove making soup, thinking what a wonderful mother Gilles would be. He was always kind and nurturing. I began to feel woozy. Something was not right. I collapsed to the ground in a heap. Moments later I came to and saw the blood on the floor.

I was lying on the examination table and Gilles was holding my hand, looking pale and worried. I tried to cheer him up but that required more energy than I could summon. My doctor came back into the room, still examining the chart. He had trouble reading his own writing, taking more than a couple of stabs at it, but finally, he figured out what he had scribbled and explained something about it being quite early in the pregnancy but the egg had wandered off target, looking for nourishment. *Of course I had a hungry unborn baby.* He added that miscarriages were sometimes the body's way of ending a pregnancy that got off to a bad start; that it was unfortunately quite a normal occurrence and that I would feel a bit of pain for a couple of days but that in a few weeks, we could try again.

I wasn't handling the loss well. I didn't want to have sex; I didn't want to do much of anything except I suddenly knew how much I wanted to have that baby. I was at loose ends and rudderless, which was bad for so many reasons. I ate whatever I saw that didn't smell bad. I had no interest in writing. Instead, I abused our dog by using her as a dress-up doll, and not with cute little cuddly-wuddly doggie clothes; I had her wearing a latex Dopey mask from Snow White. I dressed her as a Vegas showgirl, complete with sparkly bra and tassels. Poor Seeya (that was our dog's name). She was astonishingly patient and sweet with all that I did, unlike her tragically normal behavior with strangers, which varied from aloof to Cujo-like, depending on her mood.

I needed to find something constructive to do with my time besides eating, and humiliating my dog. I walked the perimeter of our home looking for something to inspire my dulled brain. I was standing in our bathroom when suddenly the lack of plushness in our towels began to matter. They were skimpy and mismatched. I moved to our bedroom, which, too, was all wrong. Our sheets had a zero thread count as far as I could see and they certainly weren't Egyptian cotton. Why that mattered bemused me; I had never cared before if they came from Latvia. Then I discovered painting, but I wasn't interested in any small canvasses. I wanted full walls. The living room was a lovely shade of Swiss cottage white, but now I wanted it to be a soft yellow. My lovely, loving, and most sainted husband of course complied. He painted the entire room—and it was a big one—yellow. But not the soft butter yellow I had in my mind and that I had described in detail as a creamy, churned butter as-if-lit-by-sunlight, yellow. What I got was more of a Velveeta-cheese-nuclear-waste kind of a yellow; a color that does not exist in nature. I wanted to be grateful. He stood in front of his masterpiece, waiting for me to jump up and down with joy. He had a big happy grin of accomplishment and a cute smear of paint on his cheek, but instead I burst into tears. I was an ungrateful bitch. Oh, what was wrong with me that I couldn't fake it?

We went to the hardware store together. I brought the exact color swatch torn from an Architectural Digest photograph of Barbara Streisand's kitchen in her Malibu house—not her Beverly Hill's house, that was more like maize; nor the marigold-yellow from her Aspen place. I wanted it exactly like the Malibu yellow, which looked like creamy churned butter!

My beautiful man repainted the whole living room all over again, but this time under my prison-warden supervision. I loved it. It was creamy, buttery yellow.

I wanted to have sex in the living room as soon as it was dry and only just a little toxic. Could it have been that a paintbrush gently sliding across my wall with just the right shade of butter yellow was making me moist? Hey, whatever it took, I was good to go.

Boom! I was once again pregnant. And I no longer gave a toss about thread count or dressing our dog in stupid outfits. Both Gilles and I were ecstatic.

For the first time in my life, I wasn't thinking about my body—except as a vessel. I was supposed to be large and round and have cravings. It was a first-time ever, wholly sanctioned time in the life of me. Total strangers came up and patted my tummy, as if giving it validation. Wow! *Hey, I had a huge belly before. Where were all of you happy tummy-thumpers back then?* I loved being pregnant. I loved the mystery in the whole blind date-ness of it all, but really, I knew it was a boy. I just knew, and I knew he'd be sweet.

Our friends and family back East wanted to give me a baby shower. We decided we had time for one more road trip before we became a threesome. I was seven months pregnant and as happy as I had ever been. I had an amazing husband who was also my best friend. It was the end of July when we set out on our cross-country drive. On the first day we burned right through blazingly hot Las Vegas and onto the north rim of the Grand Canyon where we had a hotel ready and waiting. It was close to midnight when we pulled up to the gorgeous timbered lodge and then to our cabin, which we were told stood close to the edge of one of the world's greatest views. All we could see was a black void under a canopy of stars, but we couldn't wait to see what we would wake up to in a few hours. We were both exhausted and promptly fell asleep. Twenty minutes later, I was awake, fully alert, and feeling awful. I was in the purest air I had ever been in and I couldn't breathe properly. Gilles, like a sentry, woke up and asked me what was wrong. We headed to the lodge. It was late, but there were three *dudes* flipping cards at the front desk. I explained my problem. One of them looked me over and grunted, "Uh huh." I asked what that meant.

One of the other lummoxes answered for him. "Yeah, we see a lot of that, usually it's old people; oh yeah and some pregnut ones, too." I looked at him and pointed out that I wasn't old, but if he paid any attention, he might notice I was quite *pregnut*. The third guy told me I could lose the kid unless I got off the mountain, 'cause I needed more oxygen.

Both Gilles and I became unstrung. "Is there a doctor here?"

"Nope," came the response. After several more anxiety provoking exchanges with Huey, Dewey, and Louie, I asked if there was a park ranger on site. There was, but it still hadn't occurred to any of them to call him until Gilles, scorching mad, demanded they do so.

The park ranger had me on oxygen in a heartbeat and in no uncertain terms told us we needed to go down to 5,000 feet, where I would feel far better, as would our unborn child. We were at 8,000 feet. We packed up and left immediately. It was three or four in the morning when we saw the 4,500-foot elevation sign, but another thirty minutes before we found anyplace open and with availability. We spent the rest of that night in a room at the back of a circa 1950s gas station/motel. We didn't care; I was able to breathe and our baby would be safe. I never did see the Grand Canyon.

The drive through Utah was mind-bendingly beautiful with painted rock formations in pinks, reds, and oranges, and all manner of strange-looking hoodoos—peculiar chimney-shaped rocks—protruding upward from the Badlands. They came in all shapes and sizes, from tall humans to ten-story building heights. Such weird and wonderful nature existed in very few locales; we were enthralled to be in the middle of it. The drive was primarily peaceful and by the time we started to climb the Rockies, it was as if we were seasoned pros. We pulled into the parking lot of Copper Canyon Resort and I went into the lobby in search of a park ranger who could give me oxygen. They were everywhere, carrying portable machines. I stood in front of a friendly and very cute ranger, opened my coat, and he had me hooked up in seconds. Soon I was good to go. When we got back down to the flat fields of the prairies with their endless farms of wheat and corn, I couldn't help but smile and think of my dad. "Corn, corn, corn . . . what do they do with all that bloody corn"?

My Toronto baby shower was a wonderful reminder of my other family, real and chosen, who showered us with baskets of baby clothes and sweet thoughtful gifts. Most of my time was spent being grilled about the confusion over the actual date of our marriage and whether we had really married twice. It was a bit easier explaining that it happened because my mother had willed it so, but telling the story reminded me of my crazy, headstrong, utterly amazing, and singularly unique Queen Elizabeth.

We were back home in Los Angeles after a far less eventful trip, having taken the southern route to avoid most of the big peaks. Once again, I was given a baby shower, which was not like the other in any way. First of all, one of my closest friends, Arlene, who had recently relocated to L.A. from Toronto, saw to it that all the girls were wearing, "Monica's Best Friend of the Month" T-shirts. This was all about my intense affection for whatever girl-crush I had going on whenever I made a new friend. It's true, I loved my girlfriends and considered us to be each other's Jiminy Cricket truth-tellers, to have each other's backs and be each other's backup singers, whenever necessary. To my mind there was nothing more important. A girl without girlfriends was as suspect to my mind as someone who didn't like chocolate, and a man without female friendship was just plain missing out. The excess showered upon me and my unborn child was insane, in a good way, as well as being overwhelming; I think it was, in part, because we didn't have any blood family in California that we felt so blessed with all of our surrogates.

It was hot, as only hot in October could mean in Los Angeles; dry, smoggy, and smoky from the fires burning in the hills surrounding us. My feet looked like hams. My overly pregnant tummy could be seen from space and there seemed to be a giant clock embedded in its middle. It ticked slowly and loudly but it had no desire to ring its alarm. Our baby was apparently very happy with the accommodations and had no desire to check out. The phone never stopped ringing from both coasts, everyone asking the same question: "When?" I stopped answering and left a message on the machine: "The toll bridge is closed and the baby doesn't have the correct change to be able to use the automated exit. Please send money or go away and wait like I have to!"

Two weeks later, my lovely gynecologist told me that my baby probably weighed around seven and a half pounds. He also said it was time to induce. That word did not make me happy. I liked that the kid was content; it made me feel that he already liked me. That was the upside. The downside was I was sick of peeing, creaking, and not being able to find a single comfortable position. He wanted to put me into labor right away, but in spite of my discomfort I told him I wasn't ready. He smiled knowingly; he had heard that line before. After striking a bargain that I would return by six the next morning, he let me go home to have the last supper.

As per my promise, I was back at 6 AM. Josef Mengele, my anesthesiologist, was eager to get going. He stuck a nine-foot needle in my spine, a line into my arm, and said, "Enjoy! Your baby won't put up a fight much longer." Twenty-four hours later, my kid showed him who was boss. He was staying. My gyno and Mengele had other plans. They knocked me out, made the cut, and went in . . . it *was* a boy! And he came into the world at just under eleven pounds. I wanted to put an apple in his mouth, lay him on a platter, and have a dinner for fourteen. He was the size of a Thanksgiving turkey, with hair the color of piss on snow—a vibrant day-glow yellow. His skin was pink and mottled and he had arms like German sausages. He was not what I was expecting. He was even better!

24

Jelly Belly Mama

Diets #26–29 ✦ **The Caveman Diet, Eat Nothing White Diet, Fen-Phen & The Cookie Diet**

Cost ✦ **My hair**

Weight lost ✦ **47 pounds**

Weight gained ✦ **Zero and holding**

We were parents! This was an amazing revelation that neither of us seemed able to get over. We named our son Remy. We had always wanted a French name, but one that was pronounceable, unpretentious, and hopefully easy enough to not screw up. Having a newborn was overwhelming and completely uncharted territory, especially for me. I had been around very few babies for any real length of time. But I took to nursing easily, loving the power of being someone's sole food supply. I was officially

America's Dairy-land and whenever Gilles approached, I held my hand up, "Uh uh, don't even think about it. These are no longer pleasure orbs, these are working boobs." And it never got old; it was our time, Remy's and mine. I thought about never giving my son any real food; I had no idea what one gave babies besides the stuff in those jars and nursing him was just so easy. No cooking or dishes to wash. *If I never fed him, then he wouldn't ever be fat, but of course, I'd be hauled away by child protective services.*

Gilles' mother arrived to help out. She was the loveliest, most respectful mother-in-law a girl could ever ask for; nonetheless it was the first time I had ever felt so totally lioness-like: protective, possessive, and territorial. *Back away, he's mine!* ran through my head whenever she approached. But I always handed him over, even if I didn't really want to. She had had three children and several grandchildren and knew what she was doing. She would walk him around, explaining in French what every appliance could do, naming the colors of everything they passed, and she would stop in front of every painting, telling him the story of what he was looking at. He was completely fixated on her soothing presence and completely content to be in her arms. I wished so much that my mother could have had the privilege of knowing our son. She would have loved him to pieces. She wasn't the most attentive of mothers, but she was a rock star as a grandmother.

It wasn't long before we became eligible for the "Legion of Obnoxious Parents Award." We were exhausted, sleep-deprived, and never happier. Almost everyone in Beverly Hills had a home movie theater and, seeing as we were spending all our time at home falling asleep in front of the TV or staring at our baby, we put two comfy chairs at the foot of our bed—only ours were rocking chairs—and *voila*, we had one, too. We were as obsessed with our child's development as any new parent and we couldn't shut up about him or stop comparing his virtuosity to the other babies we knew. *He always won.*

At a dinner where mostly everyone was a parent, we were all resoundingly put in our places by a couple there that didn't have children. After listening to us brag, burp our wee ones, change their diapers, and discuss descriptively what was in them, they had had enough. The husband, having anticipated this kinder-hell zone, whipped out a puppet from a bag and began rocking it and bouncing it as he and his wife shared a ten-minute litany of their puppet-child's accomplishments and bowel movements. Point taken, but we knew it wouldn't stick. *Oh my God, we had become those people . . .*

Both Gilles and I worked mostly from home and in, what had become our tradition, we turned our garage into a more useful and far prettier space—Gilles' studio. Our car was not fancy enough to be stolen and was perfectly fine parked on the street. It was California, after all, and the only weather to worry about was smog. I worked in our bedroom office and since we did have to earn a living, it meant we needed child care. Our first *au pair*, Ariane, was the twenty-one-year-old sister of one of our friends who was thrilled to leave Belgium and come and live with us. She was funny, feisty and, as a bonus, she typed. Not only did I get a great nanny, I also got an assistant.

For a small window of time I was at peace with my body, I was far too busy being one of those overly smitten and obsessed mommies I had always made fun of. Remy was now fourteen months old, walking and talking, and I was still nursing a couple of times a day. But when he stood before the dairy-bar known as me and I thought I saw him snap his little fingers and say, "Mama, booby," that was it and I was done. Our next *au pair* was German, very kind, very caring, and very homesick. I could hear her crying every night in her room. We called her mother, who sent her a ticket, and we sent her home. The timing was perfect. I was hired, along with my then-writing partner, to write an animated movie and the studios were in Dublin, Ireland. Guy and I were in Ireland, working, for about two weeks but I was having a terrible time sleeping and I couldn't concentrate. I missed my child so much that I begged the producers to let him and my husband come and join me. I promised the producers that would get so much more from *me* if *my loves* were in the same country. It wasn't that I had to be with Remy all the time, but I needed him and Gilles in the same country, in the same time zone. It was the best money they ever spent. Gilles took a leave of absence from his clients. He was never worried that they wouldn't be there when he returned. They always were. He and Remy walked Dublin while Guy and I worked, and on the weekends we explored every inch of that magical green isle. It was our last week when I was introduced, by one of the animators, to Claire, a young Irish colleen who desperately wanted to come to America. She was smart, well-educated, and loved being with Remy. We were thrilled to invite her into our home for a year. We didn't know it yet, but we were well into the parade of nations. There was a stunning Swede, a feisty Israeli, a powerhouse from

Prague, and the princess from Paris who thought it was an acting job. We sent her to a casting director and away from us.

Our cranky chow chow had become old and even crankier, and had not welcomed Remy into her life, torn between wanting to protect him or eat him. She was arthritic, plus she could no longer go up and down the stairs as she had lost her sight. We became her seeing-eye people and that was before she really started to fall apart. She had been our first "child" and it was brutal to watch her suffering. Our vet felt she was done and we had to make that awful agonizing decision to let her go. After delaying the inevitable, one day we were finally ready and had found the courage to say good-bye. We took her to the vet and watched her take her last breath. We totally forgot we were supposed to have dinner with our friends Martyn and Marcella, and when the phone began ringing over and over, we chose not to answer. But the calls were coming every five minutes so I finally picked up, barely able to speak through my sobs. Martyn was adamant that we come over for dinner as planned. He sounded annoyed; they had been cooking all day. I explained our situation, but he didn't seem to care that our dog had died that very day. I couldn't believe he was being so self-centered and hostile given the circumstances. I loved food but this was just one dinner and I was about to hang up when he shouted that we had to come over—they were throwing a surprise party for us because we were going away for the summer and their house was full of our friends!

It started far more like a wake than a party; morose and heavy-hearted with many tales of surviving near misses from our cantan-kerous dog. But soon our spirits lifted as the stories got wilder and the toasts to our dead dog got funnier and more outrageous. We stopped crying; we were doubled over with laughter despite our grief and, once again, we knew the power and gift of close friendships. By the time we got home, we were so emotionally spent from both laughing and crying that we slept better than we had in months.

By the time we got home from our summer away, I had gained weight. I tried ear stapling; it had worked for the Chinese for centuries, although it didn't work for me. The Caveman Diet just made me want to club people, and the Eat Nothing White Diet just confused me. Was that before or after Labor Day? Then I heard about Fen-Phen. (It even had a cute name.) It was the magic pill we all had been waiting for, promising that body fat would simply just fall away, as would your appetite, and it was doctor-approved. After taking just a few doses, I saw the pounds disappearing, but I also had developed a severe case of shivering. My breasts seemed perpetually cold. I went down two dress sizes in a magic minute but I couldn't shake the shakes. Everywhere I went I was complimented and admired; how could I stop? Then I saw the lead story on the evening news and it was all about the potential deadly side effects of Fen-Phen—the big one being death!

When I stopped taking the pills, I stopped shaking . . . I threw in the towel and gave up.

Our new life as parents passed in a haze of sticky fingers, Elmer's glue, birthday parties, ski outings, zoos, science centers, drums, swords, Kung Fu classes, and mountains of pizza, much of it inhaled by me.

We couldn't have been any happier until the day I almost lost my beautiful boy. We had a weekend ritual where we would drive up the coast to Gladstone's, a sprawling restaurant right on the beach. It had barrels of peanuts and the floor was covered in the crunch of their shells. It was rustic and family friendly with a million dollar view. Remy loved it. He'd order giant cups of hot chocolate that came with little paper cups filled with chocolate chips and whipped cream and he could gather up fistfuls of peanuts to feed the ever-circling seagulls. It was our place and it was perfect. After breakfast we would wander down to the beach where there were always other kids to play with. On this Saturday Remy and a feisty little girl must have played at the water's edge for nearly an hour, scooping up shells and sand in cups while the girl's mother Caroline, whom I had met once before, stood watching over them comparing notes on our children's emerging personality traits. It was a calm and typically beautiful California day when BANG! A rogue wave crashed to the shore and scooped Remy up and he was gone. My heart stopped but my legs kept moving. I ran into the water but Caroline, who was closer to him, leapt into the foamy waves with no heed to the rocks and somehow pulled him up and out—and into my arms. It all happened in a terrifying heartbeat.

I sat on the sand and cradled my little boy who kept repeating, "Mama, I'm sorry." He was in shock. I was in shock. Caroline came to see if he was okay and that's when I saw how cut up her legs were. I kept thanking her but she kept dismissing what she had done. I sat on that beach, rocking Remy for nearly thirty minutes until his body relaxed. I didn't even notice Caroline and her little girl leave. I knew I would never bump into her again and yet, this woman had saved my son's life and I didn't know how to thank her. I put Remy in his car seat and before I could shut my door, he was asleep. I turned the key and drove home, seeing nothing but the replay of that huge wave snatching my child right off the shore.

I parked the car and carried my still sleeping boy to his bed. Gilles could see by my face something was wrong but I couldn't speak. It wasn't until I sat down that I burst into tears, shaking so hard from what might have been.

It took months for Remy to let us wash his hair with the shower and years longer for him to confront swimming in a pool, let alone the ocean. It took me just as long to shake the nightmares and to let my guard down pretty much anywhere. I never took parenting for granted again. The birthday parties were another reminder that we weren't in Canada anymore: pony wranglers, reptile handlers, former Olympians, Cirque-du-Soleil acrobats, and out-of-work photojournalists taking pictures. The food, the favors, the entertainment, the outfits, the party planners, the goody bags, it was all too much. We were in need of a healthy dose of the simple life. During one summer our friend Tasha suggested we take our boys to a summer camp for both kids and adults, set in the gorgeous unspoiled wilderness of the Campbell River on Vancouver Island. What she neglected to say was that it was a camp geared toward facing one's fears and stepping out of one's comfort zone.

At first it was glorious to be together with our boys in such a stunning locale. The camp itself had a charming lodge, almost a throwback to another era, with its giant mess hall serving all the retro food one could eat, almost all of it unhealthy. There were team-building exercises and paddling in unison in giant Voyageur canoes, which were joyous expeditions along the heartbreakingly beautiful river until we stopped to set up camp. We were each given a tarp and some ludicrously thin ground-sponge that was supposed to be our bed. *I would rather have slept in a manger.* The object of the exercise was to see who could build a stable and habitable tent. Each person in our family aced this activity; I had my secret weapon Gilles, a.k.a. MacGyver, and Remy, the mini-MacGyver, as my coaches. The three of us built our shelters so quickly we even had time to adorn them with pinecones and twig wind chimes. There was some resentment that I had had help, so when it came time to build our fires, I was watched to make sure I did it on my own. Gilles and Remy could have made forty fires, they were that fast. I prayed for a lighter to fall from the sky. It didn't and I failed. We had in-depth instruction on how to avoid being carried off and eaten by bears. *That made for some sound sleeping—not!* Cliff-jumping. *That was never happening.* The ropes courses were fun for mostly everyone else; for me, they were a hell reminiscent of the Jamaica cliffs but I did them, bitching and moaning every scary step of the way.

My undoing came from a simple zip line. I was strapped and clamped within an inch of my life. It was easy enough to get to the platform but once I was there and looked down, I had a private but full-on, clammy-handed anxiety attack. I could not get off that platform, and just like back in Jamaica, I could feel the mounting pressure from the line of frustrated campers, who were now all prevented from flying off a mountain because I couldn't move. All the sweet-talking salesmanship to get me to leap was falling on my closed off ears. I was stuck. I stood there gathering sweat and realized

I was also stuck in my life. This was just another big fat metaphor. I had everything a woman could want except some missing chip that would make me lift up that one foot that was still nailed fast to the floor. I snapped out of my epiphany, sure I heard hissing behind me. I looked down and died a little more, but I had to do something, otherwise I was going to be permanently welded to this platform. One of the very hunky wilderness leaders was looking up at me imploringly. I asked him to climb up to the platform, which he did, likely in the hope that I would ask him to push me off, so that the now thirty harnessed and ready zip-liners wouldn't do it themselves.

His name was Jordy and I asked him to please look at me, in my eyes, and flirt with me as if I was his dream-girl. He looked puzzled and a touch weirded out by my request. I explained that full-on flirting was something I found quite engaging and distracting and I needed to be distracted so that I could do this. Jordy was a trooper. He locked his pretty baby-blues right on to me and went for it, as if there was no one else around. He never took his eyes off me. He was charming, funny, and really adorable and I leapt—never one to disappoint a cute guy.

Often work proved to be a great travel boon, with jobs set in exotic locales. My writing partner and I, along with our significant others, went to research the Bayou and the French Quarter as background for *All Dogs Go to Heaven* in the moody, sexy, food-filled New Orleans. New Zealand, the most open and friendly place on earth, was the location of a Ray Bradbury story in which I was cast as the last woman on Mars, desperate to hook up and marry the last man played by the incredibly talented John Glover. I wore an exact replica of Princess Diana's wedding gown, only mine had enough silk taffeta to curtain all of Buckingham Palace. I learned to love their version of Pavlova, a hard meringue filled with cream and kiwi fruit and strawberries. *I might have learned to love it too much.*

Bam! The jobs were flowing and another opportunity arose that began to plant seeds in my psyche that would take time to blossom, but it was a beginning. After several nerve-wracking auditions, I was cast as wealthy patron Mrs. Tindermarsh—a devotee of Dr. John Henry Kellogg's Battle Creek Sanitarium—in director Alan Parker's (no relation) *The Road to Wellville*. The comedy was star-packed, beginning with the amazing Sir Anthony Hopkins playing the eccentric but visionary Dr. Kellogg; it also starred John Cusack, Bridget Fonda, Matthew Broderick, Camryn Manheim, and plenty of other big names. The location was extraordinary; Mohonk Mountain House in upstate New York would have been another perfect spooky location for Stephen King to have set *The Shining*. The hotel was a huge turn of the century folly, supposedly inhabited by ghosts. For me it was akin to being invited to be part of the best, most creative summer camp in the world, nestled in the Catskill Mountains, with a gorgeous lake and so much talent. The story took place at the turn of the century and focused on Dr. Kellogg's seemingly wacky beliefs about the correct way to eat and exercise. He was so far ahead of his time.

At the Battle Creek Sanitarium, Kellogg held classes on food preparation for homemakers. Sanitarium visitors engaged in breathing exercises and mealtime marches to promote proper digestion of food throughout the day. Kellogg made sure that the bowel of each and every patient was plied with water, from above and below. Every water enema was followed by a pint of yogurt—half was eaten, the other half was administered by enema, "thus planting the protective germs where they are most needed and may render most effective service." Kellogg believed that most disease is alleviated by a change in intestinal flora; that bacteria in the intestines can either help or hinder the body; that pathogenic bacteria produce toxins during the digestion of protein that poison the blood; that a poor diet favors harmful bacteria that can then infect other tissues in the body; that the intestinal flora is changed by diet and is generally changed for the better by a well-balanced vegetarian diet favoring low-protein, laxative, and high-fiber foods.

—John Henry Kellogg, from Wikipedia

Being invited to play with that remarkable company of actors was inspirational, and even though it was far from a perfect movie, it was a gift to be a part of it and visually, it was stunning. Most inspiring was the inkling I got that Dr. Kellogg might have been a true visionary, given that here we are a century later eating and doing pretty much everything he believed was the road to health. Of course colonic has become the new word for enema. I hoped to never become familiar with either. And, I prefer my yogurt travelling south rather than his prescribed northern route.

I was sad and going through a kind of postpartum depression when the film wrapped. I had just boarded a flight back to Los Angeles, feeling a bit weepy, when an incredibly handsome man sat down beside me. Having always been a fan of the pretty, I thought I could at least get some joy from stealing quick looks at his lovely face. He spoke to me about nothing in particular but from that first minor exchange I commented on his being from Australia and that's where our nonstop conversation began. Gary was as charming and clever as he was good looking, and when the flight attendant came by to ask if we wanted a drink, Gary responded that we didn't need one. Not for a second did I feel there was anything improper or flirtatious in our tennis match-like exchange, but a couple of hours into the flight, after having shared our political, religious and social views, we were feeling pretty fortunate to be passing the time in each other's company.

Out of nowhere, Gary took my hand. In an instant I was no longer comfortable, and then he placed my hand over his heart. *Okay—getting weird* . . . "Tell me what you feel?" *Oh my, I felt a bra!* I felt my face flush but I soon recovered. "We have two hours left on this flight and I want you to think of me as Oprah and you are my only guest. What's up with the bra? Explain please." Gary told me he was a cross-dresser. He didn't know why but he loved wearing women's clothes, he always had. His wife and two daughters were not quite as thrilled. He added that his wife had left him, but his daughters were trying to find a way to accept it all. He told me he was the CEO of a very big engineering firm, and when hiring people, he would always alert them that he may appear as Gretchen at certain times. If they couldn't handle it, they should consider finding work elsewhere. I had many more questions, wanting to understand a slice of life that was completely foreign to me, but the time just flew. It seemed that we were landing only minutes after Gary's surprise confession. As we taxied to the gate I asked him what made him tell me something so personal after knowing me for such a short time? I already knew the answer. People tell me things; they always have. Gary told me he trusted me because he sensed I wasn't judgmental about the choices people made. It was true. I had never cared what people did as long as they didn't intentionally hurt others. It was none of my business. I knew a thing or two about being judged by my cover, not my content.

Gary helped me with my bags and asked if I would ever consider having dinner with him when he was dressed as his alter ego, Gretchen. Once again, the writer in me leapt at the chance. Not only did I have an appetite for food; I also loved the banquet of unique people who dared to be different.

When I told Gilles, he was awestruck at my ability to have total strangers share their deepest secrets with me and he was with me all the way. If you weren't hurting anyone, life was yours to take on in any way that brought about happiness. Then he threatened to hide behind a plant or dress as a girl and join us. Even knowing he was kidding, I refused to tell him where we were meeting. That being said, I wasn't quite prepared for "Gretchen" when I met "her" in the restaurant of my choosing, one that I was sure no one I knew went to. *Wrong!*

I was sitting in the lobby bar waiting for Gretchen to arrive, when in walked a six-foot-tall woman, wearing a really bad outfit accessorized by the largest pearly-beige shoes I had ever seen. That, and a heavy-handed makeup job, made the formerly gorgeous Gary into one really ugly woman. As we walked toward our corner, I saw a table filled with people I knew far too well to avoid. With Gretchen in tow, I took a deep breath and crossed over to say hello and to introduce my dinner companion. Gary did nothing to change his voice, but no one seemed to bat an eye. They took it all in stride; it was Los Angeles, a place filled with all kinds of fruits and nuts. We sat down and the strangest thing happened; this attractive man, who I had found so engaging, was now sitting across from me dressed as a woman and he/she began flirting with me. It was more than flirting. This man, dressed as a woman, was using his "girlfriend" intimacy chit to come on to me. This was a brain dance I couldn't get my head around. I realized Gary had taken my openness as potential for something far more. My curiosity went out the window and I was no longer into him or her. He/she had become like some weird date that I couldn't wait to get rid of: a wolf on the prowl, dressed in really bad sheep's clothing. *Aaaarghh. No thanks!* All I had wanted was a wee bit of voyeurism and a good dinner. I already had a person I loved, waiting at home for me.

That night I snuggled in bed with my husband, when at 4:31 in the morning the house began to shake violently. I remember little of the beginnings of what was soon to be called the Northridge quake, but I do remember leaping out of bed and racing to Remy's room to get him. Gilles told me later that the bookshelves lining the hall were falling, and flying books had bombarded me as I ran past, but the adrenalin protected me from feeling any of it. We huddled together in our central stairway. It was the sound I will always remember; the shaking from all around produced something like a "freight train going off its rails" kind of sound that mingled with the many car alarms, the crashing of dishes and glasses, and the brick fireplaces tumbling down. The craziness was interrupted by our ringing phone. It wasn't even close to dawn and it was my sister in Toronto wanting to make sure we were okay. How did she know? She said to turn on our television. Of course, CNN, that's how she knew: it was after seven in Toronto and she had been watching the morning news. Unbelievably, our TV still worked, even though it was now on the other side of the room. Our piano was upended, but we were okay.

We had many friends in the neighborhood and our house became the designated gathering place. By five in the morning, there were at least half a dozen neighbors all comparing notes on their jarring wake-up calls. The enormity of the quake was just beginning to sink in; it had been a 6.7 on the Richter scale. Gilles had climbed over the broken dishes and condiments and was already serving up coffee and pastries. The TV was playing in the background, and in a glance I thought I recognized a heavily decimated apartment building. I had only been there once to visit my eighty-something Uncle Arthur, my mother's brother, and his wife Erna. It looked like Godzilla had stepped on it, as it was completely pancaked. Out front stood an old couple in their pajamas, looking stunned and dazed, being interviewed by a reporter already on the scene. It was them. I was in disbelief. I heard him say they had been asleep in their second floor bedroom and then they weren't. They woke up and they were on the first floor. The one below them lay crushed with everything and everyone in it, gone. I then heard my uncle, his eyes filled with tears, speaking in shock: "We survived the hell of war and now we have to start over?" They never really recovered.

Many of our Canadian friends packed up and went back home, as did pals from as far as Great Britain and France. But we decided there were random acts of nature almost everywhere and this was our home. We weren't going anywhere.

Remy might have been a big baby, but he was a skinny little boy. Around his ninth birthday, as a not very good present, he got fat! Nothing had changed—not in his mostly vegetarian diet or active life—except the timer on his gene pool had kicked in and begun filling with the overflow of my Austro-Hungarian hormones. I felt awful. I wanted to protect him and put him in the Hansel and Gretel witch's cage and starve him. Gilles, the saner voice, thought perhaps we shouldn't draw any attention to his changing body, that it would sort itself out. *Sure, it's possible. He'll be that one happy fat kid.* He wasn't. He hated his new, large body and no matter how often I kept telling him he was the same handsome boy I had always loved, he didn't believe me. I knew Gilles was right; our son's unhappiness was not my fault but somewhere I knew my endless struggle with my weight would have to affect his and for this I was sad.

So, in my twisted body-logic I decided there shouldn't be two overweight people in the same house. It would minimize the taunting and teasing from the bullies who would soon enough begin to circle. Kids can sometimes be cruel but our son was not someone who could toss things off lightly. He was deeply sensitive and incredibly hard on himself: and having a fat mother didn't help.

I was determined to shed my body mass yet again. I found what I was sure was the magic bullet: The Cookie Diet! I loved the name and the promises, "forty pounds in forty minutes." Okay, perhaps that was a bit of an exaggeration, but they did promise the weight would just fly off. Why wouldn't it? The diet consisted of six small, and by that they meant six *tiny* protein cookies a day! Plus all the salad and nonfat dressing one could inhale. It was all very state-of-the-art. White lab coats for all the staff; scheduled visits with weigh-in's, and all kinds of highly recommended, but very pricey diet supplements on display along with their branded line of very pricey nonfat salad dressings. The cookies came in three flavors: sand, dirt, and gravel. A hamster could not have survived on this diet. But I dropped pounds by the truckload and plenty of my hair. *Why was my hair falling out?* My hairdresser explained to me I was suffering from a protein deficiency. But I lost forty pounds in two months! I went down almost three dress sizes and I had a waist. I figured I could always get a wig. Let there be dancing. Gilles threw me a party and everyone brought cake.

25

The Revolving Door

Diet #30 ✦ **Urine shots—What?**

Cost ✦ **$2,500**

Weight lost ✦ **80 pounds**

Weight gained ✦ **How much does insanity weigh?**

As Remy came through the hell of puberty, his weight fell off in the same way it had come on—fast—but mine came and went and came again and again like a badass pimp checking on his cash cow. At this point I thought it might be faster and cheaper to buy a body-babe and go in and have my head transplanted on to her body. By my last count, I had spent one million, eleven dollars, and eighty-seven cents on weight loss. *The loss part was on a sliding scale, mostly sliding upward.* Add to that the medical bills for seeking just one doctor who would tell me I had a sticky thyroid but, nope, they all concurred that my thyroid was working just fine. *I'm sure when talking amongst themselves they said it was me who wasn't working hard enough.* And I did finally go on a therapist hunt, but I really didn't want to spend fifteen years on anyone else's couch but my own—especially not to talk about my mummy and daddy issues. They were my parents and without them, where would I be? *Exactly . . . so a thank you is always in order.*

On my way home one day I noticed a giant billboard touting a special on something called Lap Band something. I was whipping by pretty quickly, so it took a moment; I thought it was a travel site promoting a trip to Lapland, maybe to visit Santa. But then I got it. It was a quick fix surgery so one could look less like Santa. I didn't want a lap band, it just sounded like some very unattractive belt. What I was really looking for was someone with a magic wand.

I grazed on Brussels sprouts, cauliflower, and colanders full of leafy greens in order that I might feel full, eat less, and drop a few pounds. What I hadn't counted on was the by-product of this misguided plan; that I wasn't hungry, just smelly. I wandered the aisles of the cookbook section in my local bookstore. I started with breakfast recipes, moved on to snacks, followed by lunch. By the time I got to the dinner recipes, I pulled up a chair to one of the lovely fake-aged tables and gorged myself with notions of chestnut-stuffed pork loin roasts with parsnips and baby potatoes, I devoured the rosemary and olive oil coated chicken breasts stuffed with Asiago cheese, accompanied by pappardelle noodles with a wild mushroom sauce. For dessert, I visually consumed all of Julia's pudding recipes, The Silver Palate's Morrocan chicken, and Joy of Cooking's chocolate mousse. I was almost sated, but I had one more stop to make, I had to bring Gilles the perfect apple pie. It was his favorite dessert, but when I walked through the door with a whole pie just for him, he pointed to his barely there, not for-real paunch and told me, my being on any food reduction plan was bad for his health, because I couldn't start feeding him instead of me. *So now the choux was on the other foot.* Day in day out, I sat in front of Oprah's Church of Divine Intervention believing her newest diet revolution would be the one. I had been on every diet she had ever been on, and they worked, just like they did for her—for a while. I fell for all the promises made by every entrant trying to get rich in the diet sweepstakes. *Sure I'll eat like bears do—all blueberries, all the time.* The lure of twenty pounds lost overnight won me over again and again. What I hadn't put together was, for every fast weight loss came a faster weight gain.

> *"The body is a very sophisticated machine that has evolved over thousands of years to deal with times of famine and drought. When you starve yourself, your body doesn't know you are trying to get skinny. It thinks there is a shortage of food and so it goes into survival mode which is a dieter's worst nightmare. Just when you think that you can trick your fat cells into shrinking more and more (to make you lose more and more weight) your body believes that there's a shortage of food . . . And if this is what your body thinks is happening, it will not let any more fat cells get smaller—in fact it will do everything it can to preserve the status quo. It does this by slowing down your metabolism."*

> —From a conversation with my GP as he tried
> to make me understand why I was wasting my time.
> And I felt it fall on my deaf ears.

Late one night, we pulled into our garage, to the half that was back to being used for car storage, and as we got out of the car, Gilles noticed a padlock on one of the storage cabinets above the car. He asked both Remy and I if either of us had locked anything inside the cupboard. We hadn't. Gilles picked up a baseball bat and knocked the lock off. When he opened the door, we were stunned to see a neatly rolled sleeping bag, a blanket, some toiletries, and food supplies. Someone was living in our garage, in a cabinet! No matter how neat and clean this person was, we really couldn't have a vagrant make his home in the garage. There were no toilets—enough said.

Gilles was removing everything when a man appeared in the driveway. He looked defeated, and even worse, familiar. We knew him. He and his wife had lived just a couple of doors down but they had gone through a messy divorce and she had the better lawyer, who had taken *him* to the cleaners. He had been a radiologist, but when his life had spiraled out of control he'd had a breakdown and lost his job. Gilles and I didn't know what to do. "Hey Harry, how you doing?" didn't feel right. We told him he could stay through the weekend. The next morning, we brought him some breakfast but he was gone.

He was the first ex-husband I had seen fall so far, so fast. I was very familiar with what happened to many of the displaced wives and mistresses, if they were unlucky enough to be tossed to the curb without enough of a cushion to get back on their feet. I also knew many great rock-solid couples in Beverly Hills, but for those other pairs on the precipice, still together but hanging by a thread, it was a very different story. None of those women, especially if they came from nothing, wanted any newly renovated, hot single ladies within 500 feet of their men. They brought fear to the neighborhood; they were threats in stilettos that had all the wives holding just a little bit tighter onto their husbands . . . and sons, if they were over fifteen. The art of shunning was alive and thriving. I asked Gilles what he would do if I ever dumped him. *As if.* He told me to go for it, but he'd be right behind me. "You can leave me, but I'm going with you." With any other human being, that might have spun me into a bout of claustrophobia, but from Gilles, it made me laugh and feel loved.

I was at the grocery store checkout, feeling up all the avocados for the guacamole I was going to make, while the other hand flipped through the latest heartaches of every celebrity called Jennifer, and I caught an ad for hCG therapy. What I really saw was: "FAT FALLS OFF OVERNIGHT!" My desperation had finally reached its apex and I fell down another rabbit hole to where the purveyors of magical thinking lived. I asked around and got tons of testimonials from less than reliable sources who were not really sure what hCG was but had heard it worked. When someone I knew whispered in my ear that there was a doctor who'd had great success with this weight-loss system, I was in, even after she told me, "hCG is comprised of daily shots from the urine of pregnant women or possibly cows." She wasn't sure which. What? But of course I made an appointment.

A very real doctor in a white coat sat behind his large and reas-suring desk and looked me over and immediately agreed I was an excellent candidate. I was happy to be excellent. He asked me how much weight I wanted to lose. I told him, "All of it."

He assured me that with just one shot every day straight into my hip, the weight would fall off. The miracle was in the pregnancy hormone that was flushed by the urine, now put to better use than having it swirl down a drain. I nodded as if any of this sounded sane. I nervously inquired how much this miracle would cost. He felt it was a bargain at $2,500 given that it was for a six-month supply, and generously added I could pay it off in installments. I took out my checkbook.

He forgot to mention that the diet that went with the shots was a mere 500 calories. *That was like two sticks of gum.* How much water-packed tuna could one be expected to eat? How much leafy green compost crap could a person mulch?

But for almost ten months, I was holed up like a prisoner unable to socialize as gathering with others seemed to always take place around a table and I needed to avoid all temptation. It was stark, monotonous, and isolating. Every day was the same: Breakfast, one piece of woody, fibery toast with a vapor trail of peanut butter; lunch was one scoop of water-packed tuna on a pile of leaves; dinner, a boneless, skinless, tasteless chicken breast with a pile of different leaves; and then, as a reward, I got a tiny bowl of sugar-free, zero-calorie, zero-taste, chemicals-in-a-cup-Jell-O-like-thingy. For the second time in my adult life I lost more than eighty pounds. Eighty pounds: that was like ten bags of fertilizer, or a twelve-year-old child. I was a mere shadow of my former self and I could officially walk on water. I wore my superiority like a bullfighter's cape, flourishing it at every opportunity. I was so much better than everyone else.

Given my current food resistance, I was in an anorexic's frame of mind when my friend Joan sent me a book she thought I might enjoy. It was called *Hunger Point* and it was a great read, about a pair of sisters with different eating disorders that wreaked havoc on their lives. The story centered on the obsessive, often destructive, relationship women have with food and dieting; it was both heartbreaking and funny and I loved it. I thought the author, Jillian Medoff, had struck a very relatable chord and I sent the book to yet another good friend of mine, Trevor Walton, who ran the television movie department at Lifetime Television. He bought it. I had sold stories to the networks before and had dipped my toe into the producing world as an associate producer—which is a euphemism for not having to do much actual work—but I had been lucky and had been schooled by a terrific woman who had allowed me to shadow her on the movies that I had brought to her. For this one, Trevor put me together with a wonderful and experienced producer he liked working with, Ellyn Williams, and we were off to the races. I was now able to add executive producer to my career path. The movie starred Barbara Hershey and the now very famous Christina Hendricks of *Mad Men*.

Producing a movie is hard work with high stress and long hours, often sixteen-hour plus days, along with the responsibility for the huge team chosen and hired by us and answerable to us, while we were answerable to the network paying the bills. But along with the hard work, there is also the kind of camaraderie formed out of intensity and shared goals. There is also a lot of downtime waiting for shots to be set up, with platters of food on offer to keep everyone's energy from flagging. It took every ounce of superhuman willpower to snack on the crudités and low fat choices while staring lustfully at the mountain of peanut butter cups, donuts, croissants, and every imaginable type of juicy finger foods. Old habits do die hard, especially when there are trays and trays of yummy, fat-producing treats shoved under my nose. I have never been a nail biter but the array of butt-enhancing deliciousness constantly on offer broke me. My old friends, cheese and chocolate, were soon screaming my name and I answered by inhaling every piece I got my hands on. The famine was over!

I fell back down that hole where my missing self was waiting to come on home. Remember fatoms? They will find you.

26

The Last Dance

Diets ✦ **1-100**

Cost ✦ **$1,000,011.87**

Weight lost ✦ **1,000 pounds**

Weight gained ✦ **Not the point**

I had no will power left. I was eating old after-dinner mints scraped from the bottom of my purse as I sat in my snobby Beverly Hills gynecologist's office for the annual spelunking expedition to make sure all systems were a go. I stared at the aquarium filled with most of the tropical fish from the part of the ocean surrounding Maui and I caught my reflection; the yo-yo cycle had run me over and killed me dead. If I hadn't quite gained back all eighty pounds, I was well on my way. I was deep into a cycle of self-loathing and fury at my weakness. I glanced at a brochure extolling the brilliance of liposuction. I picked it up then put it back down, then picked it up again. The photo of the newly lipo'd model morphed into a newly thin me, but the nurse arrived and broke the moment.

I was lying down with feet hooked into the must-be-male-designed cold-steel vagina splaying apparatus. My doctor, wearing his miner's cap, was rooting around in the dark depths of hell so, of course, I made idle conversation, inquiring about his standard poodle's well-being and about the lovely new herringbone couches in the waiting room. I believe I even commented on his tanned complexion, which led to a conversation about the joys of winter skiing—as if I had a clue—but I played along just as though we were at a cocktail party. Finally, during the removal of the icy cold speculum I said to my longtime gynecologist and advertised lipo-sucker extraordinaire, as if it were perfectly normal, "So how would we go about this lipo thing?" Faster than a speeding bullet, my feet were back on the ground and the backless paper gown was on the floor and I was stark naked. I was sure I heard him chuckling. I took a quick look at my body and thought this was hopeless but he was only too eager to demonstrate. He whipped out his special Sharpie and began to draw a never-ending series of large circles: on my hips, my buttocks, my stomach—*all of them*—on my thighs, my knees, my upper arms, my back, and on my wattle. I was standing in front of a mirror while this humiliation was taking place. My eyes were squeezed tightly shut. I'd rather have had his entire arm up my *hoohah*. He was humming. *Other images began swirling: a tube attached to me, funneling fat and grease directly into a biofuel container. Cars could run for years to come. What if he charged by the circle? I'd be thin but too broke to buy any new clothes.* He stopped humming.

My gyno/cosmetic surgeon pointed to each circle and explained how much fat would be sucked out and then, in a slightly silky used car salesman's voice, he continued explaining that the procedure was a tad expensive but then asked how many times had I starved myself for months on end, worked out till my muscles were screaming and still I was not happy with how I looked ... *Oh excuse me, show me a woman who's happy with how she looks, even when she has a great body. The whole freakin' world is a fun house mirror.* I snapped back to consciousness to hear him say I should trust him because this was the easy road to a better, thinner new me and I didn't have to do a thing—just leave the driving to him.

The procedure would only take a couple of hours; however, I would be wrapped, head-to-toe, in a mummy-esque, Ace bandage/ Spanx combo thing for a few days—a kind of vapor lock to keep the fat from trying to get back in. Doctor Lipo, however, would be back at the office, armed with his silver speculum before any of his gyno-patients had a chance to miss him. How desperate did he think fat people were? *Don't go there.* I allowed my gyno, now lipo-sucker, to seduce me with the vapor of possibility. Oh how I wanted his magic wand to work. I took out my checkbook. I was soon back in the nurse's office having blood drawn and a variety of other pre-op tests. *Alakazam!* A cancellation appeared out of thin air and I was booked for surgery two days later at seven in the morning.

I was digesting all of this while waiting for an elevator, when one of the other gynecologists, possibly a jealous one, came out of the office. He had seen me getting the blood work done and he sidled up to me as we rode down in the elevator. In no uncertain terms he told me there was a lot o' money to be made in lipo-land and he didn't approve but he felt I needed to know that this procedure was no walk in the park. "Have you ever been whacked hard with a baseball bat? This is similar; think extreme mugging!"

I was home feeling excited about my new body-to-be and terrified at the body blows I would have to endure to get it. But I gave birth to an eleven-pound boy; nothing could hurt more than that, *could it?* That baby, now fifteen, hurled himself with his giant-sized stinky shoes onto the bed where I was sitting and praying, and asked why I was doing this. The answer rolled out of me, surprising us both. I was tired of shopping in fat-girl stores, I was sick of dieting. I didn't want to be different; I wanted to blend in. Remy pointed out that I had made a whole life out of being different and he didn't believe me. I was no longer sure what I believed. I just knew I was tired of the dance. I wanted to be like Sleeping Beauty and go to bed fat and wake up thin. He looked at me, "Mom, what if you don't?" *What if I don't?*

My son had only ever known a mother who reacted to food as if it were either kryptonite or heroin. "Get that Alfredo sauce away from me. I'm getting bigger just by looking at it." "Who has candy? I gotta have some sugar. Now!" My sweet, caring boy was scared for *me* and for him.

He took a lawyer's stance and argued that it just wasn't me. "It's stupid and it's dangerous."

What did he mean by that? Crap, I knew what he meant; I was never going to be thin. They could have had those fat-sucking tubes pumping for twenty-four straight hours and I would have been thinner, but I'd still be me . . . potato me. I had lived most of my life on one diet after another as I tried to bet against the house, but the house always won. I sent flowers to my gynecologist, begging his forgiveness for cancelling, but really it was in the hope that he'd return my deposit.

I thought about Gilles and how much this man loved me, no matter what weight I was. He once asked me, "What if I was the fat one? Would you have given me a chance?" *Uh oh.* I honestly couldn't answer. Had the tables been reversed like that, I hoped I would have gone with my heart as he had, or I would have missed out on one of the most beautiful human beings on the planet. Gilles said that's how he felt about me. He hoped that one day I would see me as he did, and as my friends and family did. *I, too, prayed I would get there.*

In an odd but serendipitous way, a few days later it was our close friend Noreen's birthday and I wanted to find something unique to surprise her with. I was excited when I found a restaurant that offered a "dining in the dark" experience, which was supposed to enhance our senses of taste, smell, touch, and hearing by abandoning the one that we often take for granted—our sight.

We met in the lounge area of the restaurant, our coats were hung up, and we were handed menus and instructed to pick our dinners from a specially prepared list. Noreen, her husband Kevin, Gilles, and I were then greeted warmly by our blind server who instructed us to hold on to her and each other's shoulders as she led us led farther and farther into a pitch-black dining room. The deeper into the room we went, the more apprehensive and slightly giddy we became. We could hear conversations, punctuated by the clinking of glasses and silverware and the occasional burst of laughter, but it was completely disorienting not to know where we were going or what the room looked like. When we got to our table, our server took us one by one and had us touch the backs of our chairs in order to seat ourselves. She then told us she would be bringing the wine. "Wine!"

It was surreal and more than a little uncomfortable to be sitting in pitch black, where no matter how much you blinked, your eyes never adjusted, but our hearing became absolutely acute. There was a distinct feeling of apprehension that enveloped all of us, in spite of knowing we were in a safe place. It took a moment, but then came the joy of discovery as we groped around the table and found our utensils. I was giddy when I discovered a breadbasket filled with rolls. The scent was heady. Kevin found a little pot of butter and we collapsed in laughter when more than one of us began buttering our hands instead of the bread. Our waitress brought the wine and deftly poured it by holding the stemless glasses one at a time, then asking each of us to reach up and take it from her hands. She told us that she had not always been blind but had had meningitis as a child, which had caused her to lose her eyesight; yet she rode the buses and worked at a fast-food restaurant during the day at the takeout window. When our dinners came, we giggled, as we couldn't resist feeling everything on our plates, exclaiming with joy at the recognition of a Brussels sprout or a cherry tomato. When hands accidently touched across the table in search of salt or pepper, we became sensory explorers as we touched each other trying to figure out who was who. We could hear squeals of delight from tables around us as they made discoveries of their own. (Some sounded more than a little risqué.) The food was delicious and we decided the chefs were definitely not blind. It was a magical evening in that everything was about revelations, sensual and sensory, with an